A Prentice Hall Pocket Reader

• • • • • • • • • • • •

D0223961

PATTERNS

Edited by

Dorothy Minor

Tulsa Community College

PEARSON

Prentice
Hall

Upper Saddle River, New Jersey 07458

© 2005 by PEARSON EDUCATION, INC.
Upper Saddle River, New Jersey 07458

10 9

ISBN 0-13-225068-3

Printed in the United States of America

CONTENTS

1

NARRATION

ONLY DAUGHTER
Sandra Cisneros

Once, several years ago, when I was just starting out my writing 1
career, I was asked to write my own contributor's note for an anthology. I wrote: "I am the only daughter in a family of six sons. *That*
explains everything."

Well, I've thought that ever since, and yes, it explains a lot to me, 2
but for the reader's sake I should have written: "I am the only daughter in a *Mexican* family of six sons." Or even: "I am the only daughter of a Mexican father and a Mexican-American mother." Or: "I am
the only daughter of a working-class family of nine." All of these had
everything to do with who I am today.

I was/am the only daughter and *only* a daughter. Being an only 3
daughter in a family of six sons forced me by circumstance to spend
a lot of time by myself because my brothers felt it beneath them to
play with a *girl* in public. But that aloneness, that loneliness, was
good for a would-be writer—it allowed me time to think and think,
to imagine, to read and prepare myself.

Being only a daughter for my father meant my destiny would 4
lead me to become someone's wife. That's what he believed. But
when I was in the fifth grade and shared my plans for college with
him, I was sure he understood. I remember my father saying, *"Que
bueno, mi'ja,* that's good." That meant a lot to me, especially since my
brothers thought the idea hilarious. What I didn't realize was that my
father thought college was good for girls—good for finding a husband. After four years in college and two more in graduate school,

and still no husband, my father shakes his head even now and says I wasted all that education.

In retrospect, I'm lucky my father believed daughters were 5 meant for husbands. It meant it didn't matter if I majored in something silly like English. After all, I'd find a nice professional eventually, right? This allowed me the liberty to putter about embroidering my little poems and stories without my father interrupting with so much as a "What's that you're writing?"

But the truth is, I wanted him to interrupt. I wanted my father to 6 understand what it was I was scribbling, to introduce me as "My only daughter, the writer." Not as "This is my only daughter. She teaches." *Es maestra*—teacher. Not even *profesora.*

In a sense, everything I have ever written has been for him, to 7 win his approval even though I know my father can't read English words, even though my father's only reading includes the brown-ink *Esto* sports magazines from Mexico City and the bloody *¡Alarma!* magazines that feature yet another sighting of *La Virgen de Guadalupe* on a tortilla or a wife's revenge on her philandering husband by bashing his skull in with a *molcajete* (a kitchen mortar made of volcanic rock). Or the *fotonovelas*, the little picture paperbacks with tragedy and trauma erupting from the characters' mouths in bubbles.

A father represents, then, the public majority. A public who is dis- 8 interested in reading, and yet one whom I am writing about and for, and privately trying to woo.

When we were growing up in Chicago, we moved a lot because 9 of my father. He suffered bouts of nostalgia. Then we'd have to let go of our flat, store the furniture with mother's relatives, load the station wagon with baggage and bologna sandwiches and head south. To Mexico City.

We came back, of course. To yet another Chicago flat, another 10 Chicago neighborhood, another Catholic school. Each time, my father would seek out the parish priest in order to get a tuition break, and complain or boast: "I have seven sons."

He meant *siete hijos*, seven children, but he translated it as "sons." 11 "I have seven sons." To anyone who would listen. The Sears Roebuck employee who sold us the washing machine. The short-order cook where my father ate his ham-and-eggs breakfasts. "I have seven sons." As if he deserved a medal from the state.

My papa. He didn't mean anything by the mistranslation, I'm 12 sure. But somehow I could feel myself being erased. I'd tug my father's sleeve and whisper: "Not seven sons. Six! and one *daughter.*"

When my oldest brother graduated from medical school, he ful- 13
filled my father's dream that we study hard and use this—our heads,
instead of this—our hands. Even now my father's hands are thick
and yellow, stubbed by a history of hammer and nails and twine and
coils and springs. "Use this," my father said, tapping his head, "and
not this," showing us those hands. He always looked tired when he
said it.

Wasn't college an investment? And hadn't I spent all those years 14
in college? And if I didn't marry, what was it all for? Why would anyone go to college and then choose to be poor? Especially someone
who has always been poor.

Last year, after ten years of writing professionally, the financial 15
rewards started to trickle in. My second National Endowment for the
Arts Fellowship. A guest professorship at the University of
California, Berkeley. My book, which sold to a major New York publishing house.

At Christmas, I flew home to Chicago. The house was throbbing, 16
same as always; hot *tamales* and sweet *tamales* hissing in my mother's
pressure cooker, and everybody—my mother, six brothers, wives,
babies, aunts, cousins—talking too loud and at the same time, like in
a Fellini film, because that's just how we are.

I went upstairs to my father's room. One of my stories had just 17
been translated into Spanish and published in an anthology of
Chicano writing, and I wanted to show it to him. Ever since he recov-
ered from a stroke two years ago, my father likes to spend his leisure
hours horizontally. And that's how I found him, watching a Pedro
Infante movie on Galavision and eating rice pudding.

There was a glass filmed with milk on the bedside table. There 18
were several vials of pills and balled Kleenex. And on the floor, one
black sock and a plastic urinal that I didn't want to look at but looked
at anyway. Pedro Infante was about to burst into song, and my father
was laughing.

I'm not sure if it was because my story was translated into 19
Spanish, or because it was published in Mexico, or perhaps because
the story dealt with Tepeyac, the *colonia* my father was raised in and
the house he grew up in, but at any rate, my father punched the mute
button on his remote control and read my story.

I sat on the bed next to my father and waited. He read it very 20
slowly. As if he were reading each line over and over. He laughed at
all the right places and read lines he liked out loud. He pointed and
asked questions: "Is this So-and-so?" "Yes," I said. He kept reading.

How the Crab Apple Grew
Garrison Keillor

It has been a quiet week in Lake Wobegon. It was warm and 1
sunny on Sunday, and on Monday the flowering crab in the Dieners'
backyard burst into blossom. Suddenly, in the morning, when everyone turned their backs for a minute, the tree threw off its bathrobe
and stood trembling, purple, naked, revealing all its innermost flowers. When you saw it standing where weeks before had been a bare
stick stuck in the dirt, you had to stop; it made your head spin.

Becky Diener sat upstairs in her bedroom and looked at the tree. 2
She was stuck on an assignment from Miss Melrose for English, a
750-word personal essay, "Describe your backyard as if you were seeing it for the first time." After an hour she had thirty-nine words,
which she figured would mean she'd finish at 1:45 P.M. Tuesday, four
hours late, and therefore would get an F even if the essay was great,
which it certainly wasn't.

How can you describe your backyard as if you'd never seen it? If 3
you'd never seen it, you'd have grown up someplace else, and
wouldn't be yourself; you'd be someone else entirely, and how are
you supposed to know what that person would think?

She imagined seeing the backyard in 1996, returning home from 4
Hollywood. "Welcome Becky!" said the big white banner across
McKinley Street as the pink convertible drove slowly along, everyone clapping and cheering as she cruised by, Becky Belafonte the
movie star, and got off at her old house. "Here," she said to the
reporters, "is where I sat as a child and dreamed my dreams, under
this beautiful flowering crab. I dreamed I was a Chinese princess."
Then a reporter asked, "Which of your teachers was the most important to you, encouraging you and inspiring you?" And just then she
saw an old woman's face in the crowd, Miss Melrose pleading, whispering, "Say me, oh please, say me," and Becky looked straight at her
as she said, "Oh, there were so many, I couldn't pick out one, they
were all about the same, you know. But perhaps Miss—Miss—oh, I
can't remember her name—she taught English, I think—Miss
Milross? She was one of them. But there were so many."

She looked at her essay. "In my backyard is a tree that has always 5
been extremely important to me since I was six years old when my

dad came home one evening with this bag in the trunk and he said, 'Come here and help me plant this'—"

She crumpled the sheet of paper and started again.   6

"One evening when I was six years old, my father arrived home   7 as he customarily did around 5:30 or 6:00 P.M. except this evening he had a wonderful surprise for me, he said, as he led me toward the car.

"My father is not the sort of person who does surprising things   8 very often so naturally I was excited that evening when he said he had something for me in the car, having just come home from work where he had been. I was six years old at the time."

She took out a fresh sheet. "Six years old was a very special age   9 for me and one thing that made it special was when my dad and I planted a tree together in our backyard. Now it is grown and every spring it gives off large purple blossoms. . . ."

The tree was planted by her dad, Harold, in 1976, ten years after   10 he married her mother, Marlys. They grew up on Taft Street, across from each other, a block from the ballfield. They liked each other tremendously, and then they were in love, as much as you can be when you're so young. Thirteen and fourteen years old and sixteen and seventeen: they looked at each other a lot. She came and sat in his backyard to talk with his mother and help her shell peas but really to look at Harold as he mowed the lawn, and then he disappeared into the house and she sat waiting for him, and of course he was in the kitchen looking out at her. It's how we all began, when our parents looked at each other, as we say, "when you were just a gleam in your father's eye," or your mother's, depending on who saw who first.

Marlys was long-legged, lanky, had short black hair and sharp   11 eyes that didn't miss anything. She came over to visit the Dieners every chance she got. Her father was a lost cause, like the Confederacy, like the search for the Northwest Passage. He'd been prayed for and suffered for and fought for and spoken for, by people who loved him dearly, and when all was said and done, he just reached for the gin bottle and said, "I don't know what you're talking about," and he didn't. He was a sore embarrassment to Marlys, a clown, a joke, and she watched Harold for evidence that he wasn't similar. One night she dropped in at the Dieners' and came upon a party where Harold, now nineteen, and his friends were drinking beer by the pail. Harold flopped down on his back and put his legs in the air and a pal put a lit match up to Harold's rear end and blue flame came out like a blowtorch, and Marlys went home disgusted and didn't speak to him for two years.

Harold went crazy. She graduated from high school and started 12 attending dances with a geography teacher named Stu Jasperson, who was tall and dark-haired, a subscriber to *Time* magazine, educated at Saint Cloud Normal School, and who flew a red Piper Cub airplane. Lake Wobegon had no airstrip except for Tollerud's pasture, so Stu kept his plane in Saint Cloud. When he was en route to and from the plane was almost the only time Harold got to see Marlys and try to talk sense into her. But she was crazy about Stu the aviator, not Harold the hardware clerk, and in an hour Stu came buzzing overhead doing loops and dives and dipping his wings. Harold prayed for him to crash. Marlys thought Stu was the sun and the moon; all Harold could do was sit and watch her, in the backyard, staring up, her hand shielding her eyes, saying, "Oh, isn't he marvelous?" as Stu performed aerial feats and then shut off the throttle and glided overhead singing "Vaya con Dios" to her. "Yes, he is marvelous," said Harold, thinking, "DIE DIE DIE."

That spring, Marlys was in charge of the Sweethearts Banquet at 13 the Lutheran church. Irene Holm had put on a fancy winter Sweethearts Banquet with roast lamb, and Marlys wanted to top her and serve roast beef with morel mushrooms, a first for a church supper in Lake Wobegon. Once Irene had referred to Marlys's dad as a lush.

Morel mushrooms are a great delicacy. They are found in the 14 wild by people who walk fifteen miles through the woods to get ten of them and then never tell the location to a soul, not even on their deathbeds to a priest. So Marlys's serving them at the banquet would be like putting out emeralds for party favors. It would blow Irene Holm out of the water and show people that even if Marlys's dad was a lush, she was still someone to be reckoned with.

Two men felt the call to go and search for morels: Harold put on 15 his Red Wing boots and knapsack and headed out one evening with a flashlight. He was in the woods all night. Morels are found near the base of the trunk of a dead elm that's been dead three years, which you can see by the way moonlight doesn't shine on it, and he thought he knew where some were, but around midnight he spotted a bunch of flashlights behind him, a posse of morelists bobbing along on his trail, so he veered off and hiked five miles in the wrong direction to confuse them, and by then the sun was coming up so he went home to sleep. He woke at 2:00 P.M., hearing Stu flying overhead, and in an instant he knew. Dead elms! Of course! Stu could spot them from the air, send his ground crew to collect them for Marlys, and the Sweethearts Banquet would be their engagement dinner.

Stu might have done just that, but he wanted to put on a show 16
and land the Cub in Lake Wobegon. He circled around and around,
and came in low to the west of town, disappearing behind the trees.
"He's going to crash!" cried Marlys, and they all jumped in their cars
and tore out, expecting to find the young hero lying bloody and torn
in the dewy grass, with a dying poem on his lips. But there he was
standing tall beside the craft, having landed successfully in a field of
spring wheat. They all mobbed around him, and he told how he was
going up to find the morels and bring them back for Marlys.

There were about forty people there. They seemed to enjoy it, so 17
he drew out his speech, talking about the lure of aviation and his boyhood and various things so serious that he didn't notice Harold
behind him by the plane or notice the people who noticed what
Harold was doing and laughed. Stu was too inspired to pay attention
to the laughter. He talked about how he once wanted to fly to see the
world but once you get up in the air you can see that Lake Wobegon
is the most beautiful place of all, a lot of warm horse manure like that,
and then he gave them a big manly smile and donned his flying cap
and scarf and favored them with a second and third smile and a wave,
and he turned and there was Harold to help him into the cockpit.

"Well, thanks," said Stu, "mighty kind, mighty kind." Harold 18
jumped to the propeller and threw it once and twice, and the third
time the engine fired, and Stu adjusted the throttle, checked the
gauges, flapped the flaps, fit his goggles, and never noticed the
ground was wet and his wheels were sunk in. He'd parked in a wet
spot, and then during his address someone had gone around and
made it wetter, so when Stu pulled back on the throttle the Cub just
sat, and he gave it more juice and she creaked a little, and he gave
it more and the plane stood on its head with its tail in the air and
dug in.

It pitched forward like the *Titanic*, and the propeller in the mud 19
sounded like he'd eaten too many green apples. The door opened
and Stu climbed out, trying to look dignified and studious as he
tilted eastward and spun, and Harold said, "Stu, we didn't say we
wanted those mushrooms sliced."

Harold went out that afternoon and collected five hundred morel 20
mushrooms around one dead elm tree. Marlys made her mark at the
Sweethearts dinner, amazing Irene Holm, who had thought Marlys
was common. Harold also brought out of the woods a bouquet of
flowering crab apple and asked her to marry him, and eventually she
decided to.

The tree in the backyard came about a few years afterward. 21
They'd been married awhile, had two kids, and some of the gloss had
worn off their life, and one afternoon, Harold, trying to impress his
kids and make his wife laugh, jumped off the garage roof, pretending he could fly, and landed wrong, twisting his ankle. He lay in pain,
his eyes full of tears, and his kids said, "Oh poor Daddy, poor
Daddy," and Marlys said, "You're not funny, you're ridiculous."

He got up on his bum ankle and went in the woods and got her 22
a pint of morels and a branch from the flowering crab apple. He cut
a root from another crab apple and planted the root in the ground.
"Look, kids," he said. He sharpened the branch with his hatchet and
split the root open and stuck the branch in and wrapped a cloth
around it and said, "Now, there, that will be a tree." They said,
"Daddy, will that really be a tree?" He said, "Yes." Marlys said,
"Don't be ridiculous."

He watered it and tended it and, more than that, he came out late 23
at night and bent down and said, "GROW. GROW. GROW." The graft
held, it grew, and one year it was interesting, and the next it was
impressive and then wonderful, and finally it was magnificent. It's
the most magnificent thing in the Dieners' backyard. Becky finished
writing 750 words late that night and lay down to sleep. A backyard
is a novel about us, and when we sit there on a summer day, we hear
the dialogue and see the characters.

SHOOTING AN ELEPHANT

George Orwell

In Moulmein, in lower Burma, I was hated by large numbers of people—the only time in my life that I have been important enough for this to happen to me. I was sub-divisional police officer of the town, and in an aimless, petty kind of way anti-European feeling was very bitter. No one had the guts to raise a riot, but if a European woman went through the bazaars alone somebody would probably spit betel juice over her dress. As a police officer I was an obvious target and was baited whenever it seemed safe to do so. When a nimble Burman tripped me up on the football field and the referee (another Burman) looked the other way, the crowd yelled with hideous laughter. This happened more than once. In the end the sneering yellow faces of young men that met me everywhere, the insults hooted after me when I was at a safe distance, got badly on my nerves. The young Buddhist priests were the worst of all. There were several thousands of them in the town and none of them seemed to have anything to do except stand on street corners and jeer at Europeans.

All this was perplexing and upsetting. For at that time I had already made up my mind that imperialism was an evil thing and the sooner I chucked up my job and got out of it the better. Theoretically—and secretly, of course—I was all for the Burmese and all against their oppressors, the British. As for the job I was doing, I hated it more bitterly than I can perhaps make clear. In a job like that you see the dirty work of Empire at close quarters. The wretched prisoners huddling in the stinking cages of the lock-ups, the grey, cowed faces of the long-term convicts, the scarred buttocks of the men who had been flogged with bamboos—all these oppressed me with an intolerable sense of guilt. But I could get nothing into perspective. I was young and ill-educated and I had had to think out my problems in the utter silence that is imposed on every Englishman in the East. I did not even know that the British Empire is dying, still less did I know that it is a great deal better than the younger empires that are going to supplant it.[1] All I knew was that I was stuck between my hatred of the empire I served and my rage against the evil-spirited little beasts who tried to make my job impossible. With

---

[1] This essay was written in 1936, three years before the start of World War II; Stalin and Hitler were in power.

one part of my mind I thought of the British Raj[2] as an unbreakable tyranny, as something clamped down, in *saecula saeculorum*,[3] upon the will of prostrate peoples; with another part I thought that the greatest joy in the world would be to drive a bayonet into a Buddhist priest's guts. Feelings like these are the normal by-products of imperialism; ask any Anglo-Indian official, if you can catch him off duty.

One day something happened which in a roundabout way was 3 enlightening. It was a tiny incident in itself, but it gave me a better glimpse than I had had before of the real nature of imperialism—the real motives for which despotic governments act. Early one morning the sub-inspector at a police station the other end of the town rang me up on the phone and said that an elephant was ravaging the bazaar. Would I please come and do something about it? I did not know what I could do, but I wanted to see what was happening and I got on to a pony and started out. I took my rifle, an old .44 Winchester and much too small to kill an elephant, but I thought the noise might be useful in *terrorem*. Various Burmans stopped me on the way and told me about the elephant's doings. It was not, of course, a wild elephant, but a tame one which had gone "must." It had been chained up, as tame elephants always are when their attack of "must"[4] is due, but on the previous night it had broken its chain and escaped. Its mahout,[5] the only person who could manage it when it was in that state, had set out in pursuit, but had taken the wrong direction and was now twelve hours' journey away, and in the morning the elephant had suddenly reappeared in the town. The Burmese population had no weapons and were quite helpless against it. It had already destroyed somebody's bamboo hut, killed a cow, and raid-ed some fruit-stalls and devoured the stock; also it had met the municipal rubbish van and, when the driver jumped out and took to his heels, had turned the van over and inflicted violences upon it.

The Burmese sub-inspector and some Indian constables were 4 waiting for me in the quarter where the elephant had been seen. It was a very poor quarter, a labyrinth of squalid bamboo huts, thatched with palm-leaf, winding all over a steep hillside. I remember that it was a cloudy, stuffy morning at the beginning of the rains. We began questioning the people as to where the elephant had gone and, as usual,

---

[2] Sovereignty.
[3] From time immemorial.
[4] Frenzy.
[5] Keeper.

failed to get any definite information. That is invariably the case in the
East; a story always sounds clear enough at a distance, but the nearer
you get to the scene of events the vaguer it becomes. Some of the people said that the elephant had gone in one direction, some said that he
had gone in another, some professed not even to have heard of any elephant. I had almost made up my mind that the whole story was a pack
of lies, when we heard yells a little distance away. There was a loud,
scandalized cry of "Go away, child! Go away this instant!" and an old
woman with a switch in her hand came round the corner of a hut, vio-
lently shooing away a crowd of naked children. Some more women
followed, clicking their tongues and exclaiming; evidently there was
something that the children ought not to have seen. I rounded the hut
and saw a man's dead body sprawling in the mud. He was an Indian,
a black Dravidian coolie,[6] almost naked, and he could not have been
dead many minutes. The people said that the elephant had come suddenly upon him round the corner of the hut, caught him with its trunk,
put its foot on his back, and ground him into the earth. This was the
rainy season and the ground was soft, and his face had scored a trench
a foot deep and a couple of yards long. He was lying on his belly with
arms crucified and head sharply twisted to one side. His face was
coated with mud, the eyes wide open, the teeth bared and grinning
with an expression of unendurable agony. (Never tell me, by the way,
that the dead look peaceful. Most of the corpses I have seen looked
devilish.) The friction of the great beast's foot had stripped the skin
from his back as neatly as one skins a rabbit. As soon as I saw the dead
man I sent an orderly to a friend's house nearby to borrow an elephant
rifle. I had already sent back the pony, not wanting it to go mad with
fright and throw me if it smelt the elephant.

The orderly came back in a few minutes with a rifle and five car-   5
tridges, and meanwhile some Burmans had arrived and told us that
the elephant was in the paddy fields below, only a few hundred
yards away. As I started forward practically the whole population of
the quarter flocked out of the houses and followed me. They had
seen the rifle and were all shouting excitedly that I was going to
shoot the elephant. They had not shown much interest in the elephant when he was merely ravaging their homes, but it was different
now that he was going to be shot. It was a bit of fun to them, as it
would be to an English crowd; besides they wanted the meat. It made

---

[6] An unskilled laborer.

me vaguely uneasy. I had no intention of shooting the elephant—I had merely sent for the rifle to defend myself if necessary—and it is always unnerving to have a crowd following you. I marched down the hill, looking and feeling a fool, with the rifle over my shoulder and an ever-growing army of people jostling at my heels. At the bottom, when you got away from the huts, there was a metalled road and beyond that a miry waste of paddy fields a thousand yards across, not yet ploughed but soggy from the first rains and dotted with coarse grass. The elephant was standing eight yards from the road, his left side towards us. He took not the slightest notice of the crowd's approach. He was tearing up bunches of grass, beating them against his knees to clean them and stuffing them into his mouth.

I had halted on the road. As soon as I saw the elephant I knew with perfect certainty that I ought not to shoot him. It is a serious matter to shoot a working elephant—it is comparable to destroying a huge and costly piece of machinery—and obviously one ought not to do it if it can possibly be avoided. And at that distance, peacefully eating, the elephant looked no more dangerous than a cow. I thought then and I think now that his attack of "must" was already passing off; in which case he would merely wander harmlessly about until the mahout came back and caught him. Moreover, I did not in the least want to shoot him. I decided that I would watch him for a little while to make sure that he did not turn savage again, and then go home.

But at that moment I glanced round at the crowd that had followed me. It was an immense crowd, two thousand at the least and growing every minute. It blocked the road for a long distance on either side. I looked at the sea of yellow faces above the garish clothes—faces all happy and excited over this bit of fun, all certain that the elephant was going to be shot. They were watching me as they would watch a conjurer about to perform a trick. They did not like me, but with the magical rifle in my hands I was momentarily worth watching. And suddenly I realized that I should have to shoot the elephant after all. The people expected it of me and I had got to do it; I could feel their two thousand wills pressing me forward, irresistibly. And it was at this moment, as I stood there with the rifle in my hands, that I first grasped the hollowness, the futility of the white man's dominion in the East. Here was I, the white man with his gun, standing in front of the unarmed native crowd—seemingly the leading actor of the piece; but in reality I was only an absurd puppet pushed to and fro by the will of those yellow faces behind. I perceived in this moment that when the white man turns tyrant it is his own freedom that he destroys. He becomes a sort of hollow, posing dummy, the conventionalized figure of a sahib.[7] For it is the condition of his rule that he shall spend his life in trying to impress the "natives," and so in every crisis he has got to do what the "natives" expect of him. He wears a mask, and his face grows to fit it. I had got to shoot the elephant. I had committed myself to doing it when I sent for the rifle. A sahib has got to act like a sahib; he has got to appear resolute, to know his own mind and do definite things. To come all that way, rifle in hand, with two thousand people marching at my heels, and then to trail feebly away, having done nothing—no, that was impossible. The crowd would laugh at me. And my whole life, every white man's life in the East, was one long struggle not to be laughed at.

But I did not want to shoot the elephant. I watched him beating 8 his bunch of grass against his knees, with that preoccupied grandmotherly air that elephants have. It seemed to me that it would be murder to shoot him. At that age I was not squeamish about killing animals, but I had never shot an elephant and never wanted to. (Somehow it always seems worse to kill a *large* animal.) Besides, there was the beast's owner to be considered. Alive, the elephant was worth at least a hundred pounds; dead, he would only be worth the value of his tusks, five pounds, possibly. But I had got to act quickly. I turned to some experienced looking Burmans who had been there when we arrived, and asked them how the elephant had been behaving. They all said the same thing: he took no notice of you if you left him alone, but he might charge if you went too close to him.

It was perfectly clear to me what I ought to do. I ought to walk 9 up to within, say, twenty-five yards of the elephant and test his behavior. If he charged, I could shoot; if he took no notice of me, it would be safe to leave him until the mahout came back. But also I knew that I was going to do no such thing. I was a poor shot with a rifle and the ground was soft mud into which one would sink at every step. If the elephant charged and I missed him, I should have about as much chance as a toad under a steam-roller. But even then I was not thinking particularly of my own skin, only of the watchful yellow faces behind. For at that moment, with the crowd watching me, I was not afraid in the ordinary sense, as I would have been if I had been alone. A white man mustn't be frightened in front of "natives"; and so, in general, he isn't frightened. The sole thought in my mind was that if anything went wrong those two thousand Burmans would see me pursued, caught, trampled on, and reduced

---

[7] Term used by natives of colonial India when referring to a European of rank.

to a grinning corpse like that Indian up the hill. And if that happened it was quite probable that some of them would laugh. That would never do. There was only one alternative. I shoved the cartridges into the magazine and lay down on the road to get a better aim.

The crowd grew very still, and a deep, low, happy sigh, as of people who see the theatre curtain go up at last, breathed from innumerable throats. They were going to have their bit of fun after all. The rifle was a beautiful German thing with cross-hair sights. I did not then know that in shooting an elephant one would shoot to cut an imaginary bar running from ear-hole to ear-hole. I ought, therefore, as the elephant was sideways on, to have aimed straight at his ear-hole; actually I aimed several inches in front of this, thinking the brain would be further forward. 10

When I pulled the trigger I did not hear the bang or feel the kick—one never does when a shot goes home—but I heard the devilish roar of glee that went up from the crowd. In that instant, in too short a time, one would have thought, even for the bullet to get there, a mysterious, terrible change had come over the elephant. He neither stirred nor fell, but every line of his body had altered. He looked suddenly stricken, shrunken, immensely old, as though the frightful impact of the bullet had paralysed him without knocking him down. At last, after what seemed a long time—it might have been five seconds, I dare say—he sagged flabbily to his knees. His mouth slobbered. An enormous senility seemed to have settled upon him. One could have imagined him thousands of years old. I fired again into the same spot. At the second shot he did not collapse but climbed with desperate slowness to his feet and stood weakly upright, with legs sagging and head dropping. I fired a third time. That was the shot that did for him. You could see the agony of it jolt his whole body and knock the last remnant of strength from his legs. But in falling he seemed for a moment to rise, for as his hind legs collapsed beneath him he seemed to tower upward like a huge rock toppling, his trunk reaching skywards like a tree. He trumpeted, for the first and only time. And then down he came, his belly towards me, with a crash that seemed to shake the ground even where I lay. 11

I got up. The Burmans were already racing past me across the mud. It was obvious that the elephant would never rise again, but he was not dead. He was breathing very rhythmically with long rattling gasps, his great mound of a side painfully rising and falling. His mouth was wide open—I could see far down into caverns of pale pink throat. I waited a long time for him to die, but his breathing did not weaken. Finally I fired my two remaining shots into the spot 12 where I thought his heart must be. The thick blood welled out of him like red velvet, but still he did not die. His body did not even jerk when the shots hit him, the tortured breathing continued without a pause. He was dying, very slowly and in great agony, but in some world remote from me where not even a bullet could damage him further. I felt that I had got to put an end to that dreadful noise. It seemed dreadful to see the great beast lying there, powerless to move and yet powerless to die, and not even to be able to finish him. I sent back for my small rifle and poured shot after shot into his heart and down his throat. They seemed to make no impression. The tortured gasps continued as steadily as the ticking of a clock.

In the end I could not stand it any longer and went away. I heard later that it took him half an hour to die. Burmans were bringing dahs[8] and baskets even before I left, and I was told they had stripped his body almost to the bones by the afternoon. 13

Afterwards, of course, there were endless discussions about the shooting of the elephant. The owner was furious, but he was only an Indian and could do nothing. Besides, legally I had done the right thing, for a mad elephant has to be killed, like a mad dog, if its owner fails to control it. Among the Europeans opinion was divided. The older men said I was right, the younger men said it was a damn shame to shoot an elephant for killing a coolie, because an elephant was worth more than any damn Coringhee coolie. And afterwards I was very glad that the coolie had been killed; it put me legally in the right and it gave me a sufficient pretext for shooting the elephant. I often wondered whether any of the others grasped that I had done it solely to avoid looking a fool. 14

---

[8] Large knives.

2

DESCRIPTION

IN THE KITCHEN
Henry Louis Gates Jr.

We always had a gas stove in the kitchen, though electric cooking became fashionable in Piedmont, like using Crest toothpaste rather than Colgate, or watching Huntley and Brinkley rather than Walter Cronkite. But for us it was gas, Colgate, and good ole Walter Cronkite, come what may. We used gas partly out of loyalty to Big Mom, Mama's mama, because she was mostly blind and still loved to cook, and she could feel her way better with gas than with electric. 1

But the most important thing about our gas-equipped kitchen was that Mama used to do hair there. She had a "hot comb"—a fine-toothed iron instrument with a long wooden handle—and a pair of iron curlers that opened and closed like scissors: Mama would put them into the gas fire until they glowed. You could smell those prongs heating up. 2

I liked what that smell meant for the shape of my day. There was an intimate warmth in the women's tones as they talked with my mama while she did their hair. I knew what the women had been through to get their hair ready to be "done," because I would watch Mama do it to herself. How that scorched kink could be transformed through grease and fire into a magnificent head of wavy hair was a miracle to me. Still is. 3

Mama would wash her hair over the sink, a towel wrapped round her shoulders, wearing just her half-slip and her white bra. (We had no shower until we moved down Rat Tail Road into Doc Wolverton's house, in 1954.) After she had dried it, she would grease her scalp thoroughly with blue Bergamot hair grease, which came in a short, fat jar with a picture of a beautiful colored lady on it. It's 4 important to grease your scalp real good, my mama would explain, to keep from burning yourself.

Of course, her hair would return to its natural kink almost as soon as the hot water and shampoo hit it. To me, it was another miracle how hair so "straight" would so quickly become kinky again once it even approached some water.

My mama had only a few "clients" whose heads she "did"—and did, I think, because she enjoyed it, rather than for the few dollars it brought in. They would sit on one of our red plastic kitchen chairs, the kind with the shiny metal legs, and brace themselves for the process. Mama would stroke that red-hot iron, which by this time had been in the gas fire for half an hour or more, slowly but firmly through their hair, from scalp to strand's end. It made a scorching, crinkly sound, the hot iron did, as it burned its way through damp kink, leaving in its wake the straightest of hair strands, each of them standing up long and tall but drooping at the end, like the top of a heavy willow tree. Slowly, steadily, with deftness and grace, Mama's hands would transform a round mound of Odetta kink into a darkened swamp of everglades. The Bergamot made the hair shiny; the heat of the hot iron gave it a brownish-red cast. Once all the hair was as straight as God allows kink to get, Mama would take the well-heated curling iron and twirl the straightened strands into more or less loosely wrapped curls. She claimed that she owed her strength and skill as a hairdresser to her wrists, and her little finger would poke out the way it did when she sipped tea. Mama was a southpaw, who wrote upsidedown and backwards to produce the cleanest, roundest letters you've ever seen.

The "kitchen" she would all but remove from sight with a pair of shears bought for this purpose. Now, the *kitchen* was the room in which we were sitting, the room where Mama did hair and washed clothes, and where each of us bathed in a galvanized tub. But the word has another meaning, and the "kitchen" I'm speaking of now is the very kinky bit of hair at the back of the head, where the neck meets the shirt collar. If there ever was one part of our African past that resisted assimilation, it was the kitchen. No matter how hot the iron, no matter how powerful the chemical, no matter how stringent the mashed-potatoes-and-lye formula of a man's "process," neither God nor woman nor Sammy Davis, Jr., could straighten the kitchen. The kitchen was permanent, irredeemable, invincible kink. Unassimilably African. No matter what you did, no matter how hard you tried, nothing could dekink a person's kitchen. So you trimmed it off as best you could.

When hair had begun to "turn," as they'd say, or return to its nat- 8
ural kinky glory, it was the kitchen that turned first. When the
kitchen started creeping up the back of the neck, it was time to get
your hair done again. The kitchen around the back, and nappy edges
at the temples.

Sometimes, after dark, Mr. Charlie Carroll would come to have 9
his hair done. Mr. Charlie Carroll was very light-complected and had
a ruddy nose, the kind of nose that made me think of Edmund
Gwenn playing Kris Kringle in *Miracle on 34th Street*. At the beginning, they did it after Rocky and I had gone to sleep. It was only later
that we found out he had come to our house so Mama could iron his
hair—not with a hot comb and curling iron but with our very own
Proctor-Silex steam iron. For some reason, Mr. Charlie would conceal
his Frederick Douglass mane under a big white Stetson hat, which I
never saw him take off. Except when he came to our house, late at
night, to have his hair pressed.

(Later, Daddy would tell us about Mr. Charlie's most prized 10
piece of knowledge, which the man would confide only after his hair
had been pressed, as a token of intimacy. "Not many people know
this," he'd say in a tone of circumspection, "but George Washington
was Abraham Lincoln's daddy." Nodding solemnly, he'd add the
clincher: "A white man told me." Though he was in dead earnest, this
became a humorous refrain around the house—a "white man told
me"—used to punctuate especially preposterous assertions.)

My mother furtively examined my daughters' kitchens when- 11
ever we went home for a visit in the early eighties. It became a game
between us. I had told her not to do it, because I didn't like the politics it suggested of "good" and "bad" hair. "Good" hair was straight.
"Bad" hair was kinky. Even in the late sixties, at the height of Black
Power, most people could not bring themselves to say "bad" for
"good" and "good" for "bad." They still said that hair like white hair
was "good," even if they encapsulated it in a disclaimer like "what
we used to call 'good.' "

Maggie would be seated in her high chair, throwing food this 12
way and that, and Mama would be cooing about how cute it all was,
remembering how I used to do the same thing, and wondering
whether Maggie's flinging her food with her left hand meant that she
was going to be a southpaw too. When my daughter was just about
covered with Franco-American SpaghettiOs, Mama would seize the
opportunity and wipe her clean, dipping her head, tilted to one side,
down under the back of Maggie's neck. Sometimes, if she could get
away with it, she'd even rub a curl between her fingers, just to make

sure that her bifocals had not deceived her. Then she'd sigh with satisfaction and relief, thankful that her prayers had been answered. No kink . . . yet. "Mama!" I'd shout, pretending to be angry. (Every once in a while, if no one was looking, I'd peek too.)

I say "yet" because most black babies are born with soft, silken 13 hair. Then, sooner or later, it begins to "turn," as inevitably as do the seasons or the leaves on a tree. And if it's meant to turn, it *turns*, no matter how hard you try to stop it. People once thought baby oil would stop it. They were wrong.

Everybody I knew as a child wanted to have good hair. You 14 could be as ugly as homemade sin dipped in misery and still be thought attractive if you had good hair. Jesus Moss was what the girls at Camp Lee, Virginia, had called Daddy's hair during World War II. I know he played that thick head of hair for all it was worth, too. Still would, if he could.

My own hair was "not a bad grade," as barbers would tell me 15 when they cut my head for the first time. It's like a doctor reporting the overall results of the first full physical that he has given you. "You're in good shape" or "Blood pressure's kind of high; better cut down on salt."

I spent much of my childhood and adolescence messing with my 16 hair. I definitely wanted straight hair. Like Pop's.

When I was about three, I tried to stick a wad of Bazooka bubble 17 gum to that straight hair of his. I suppose what fixed that memory for me is the spanking I got for doing so: he turned me upside down, holding me by my feet, the better to paddle my behind. Little *nigger*, he shouted, walloping away. I started to laugh about it two days later, when my behind stopped hurting.

When black people say "straight," of course, they don't usually 18 mean "straight" literally, like, say, the hair of Peggy Lipton (the white girl on The Mod Squad) or Mary of Peter, Paul, and Mary fame; black people call that "stringy" hair. No, "straight" just means not kinky, no matter what contours the curl might take. Because Daddy had straight hair, I would have done *anything* to have straight hair—and I used to try everything to make it straight, short of getting a process, which only riffraff were dumb enough to do.

Of the wide variety of techniques and methods I came to master 19 in the great and challenging follicle prestidigitation, almost all had two things in common: a heavy, oil-based grease and evenly applied pressure. It's no accident that many of the biggest black companies in the fifties and sixties made hair products. Indeed, we do have a vast array of hair grease. And I have tried it all, in search of that certain silky touch, one that leaves neither the hand nor the pillow sullied by grease.

I always wondered what Frederick Douglass put on *his* hair, or 20 Phillis Wheatley. Or why Wheatley has that rag on her head in the little engraving in the frontispiece of her book. One thing is for sure: you can bet that when Wheatley went to England to see the Countess of Huntington, she did not stop by the Queen's Coiffeur on the way. So many black people still get their hair straightened that it's a wonder we don't have a national holiday for Madame C. J. Walker, who invented the process for straightening kinky hair, rather than for Dr. King. Jheri-curled or "relaxed"—it's still fried hair.

I used all the greases, from sea-blue Bergamot, to creamy vanilla 21 Duke (in its orange-and-white jar), to the godfather of grease, the formidable Murray's. Now, Murray's was some *serious* grease. Whereas Bergamot was like oily Jell-O and Duke was viscous and sickly sweet, Murray's was light brown and *hard*. Hard as lard and twice as greasy, Daddy used to say whenever the subject of Murray's came up. Murray's came in an orange can with a screw-on top. It was so hard that some people would put a match to the can, just to soften it and make it more manageable. In the late sixties, when Afros came into style, I'd use Afro-Sheen. From Murray's to Duke to Afro-Sheen: that was my progression in black consciousness.

We started putting hot towels or washrags over our greased- 22 down, Murray's-coated heads, in order to melt the wax into the scalp and follicles. Unfortunately, the wax had a curious habit of running down your neck, ears, and forehead. Not to mention your pillowcase.

Another problem was that if you put two palmfuls of Murray's 23 on your head, your hair turned white. Duke did the same thing. It was a challenge: if you got rid of the white stuff, you had a magnificent head of wavy hair. Murray's turned kink into waves. Lots of waves. Frozen waves. A hurricane couldn't have blown those waves around.

That was the beauty of it. Murray's was so hard that it froze your 24 hair into the wavy style you brushed it into. It looked really good if you wore a part. A lot of guys had parts *cut* into their hair by a barber, with clippers or a straight-edge razor. Especially if you had kinky hair—in which case you'd generally wear a short razor cut, or what we called a Quo Vadis.

Being obsessed with our hair, we tried to be as innovative as pos- 25 sible. Everyone knew about using a stocking cap, because your father or your uncle or the older guys wore them whenever something really big was about to happen, secular or sacred, a funeral or a dance, a wedding or a trip in which you confronted official white people, or when you were trying to look really sharp. When it was time to be clean, you wore a stocking cap. If the event was really a big one, you made a new cap for the occasion.

A stocking cap was made by asking your mother for one of her   26
hose, and cutting it with a pair of scissors about six inches or so from the open end, where the elastic goes up to the top of the thigh. Then you'd knot the cut end, and behold—a conical-shaped hat or cap, with an elastic band that you pulled down low on your forehead and down around your neck in the back. A good stocking cap, to work well, had to fit tight and snug, like a press. And it had to fit that tightly because it *was* a press: it pressed your hair with the force of the hose's elastic. If you greased your hair down real good and left the stocking cap on long enough—*voilà:* you got a head of pressed-against-the-scalp waves. If you used Murray's, and if you wore a stocking cap to sleep, you got a *whole lot* of waves. (You also got a ring around your forehead when you woke up, but eventually that disappeared.)

And then you could enjoy your concrete 'do. Swore we were bad,   27
too, with all that grease and those flat heads. My brother and I would brush it out a bit in the morning, so it would look—ahem—"natural."

Grown men still wear stocking caps, especially older men, who   28
generally keep their caps in their top drawer, along with their cuff links and their see-through silk socks, their Maverick tie, their silk handkerchief, and whatever else they prize most.

A Murrayed-down stocking cap was the respectable version of   29
the process, which, by contrast, was most definitely not a cool thing to have, at least if you weren't an entertainer by trade.

Zeke and Keith and Poochie and a few other stars of the basket-   30
ball team all used to get a process once or twice a year. It was expensive, and to get one you had to go to Pittsburgh or D.C. or Uniontown, someplace where there were enough colored people to support a business. They'd disappear, then reappear a day or two later, strutting like peacocks, their hair burned slightly red from the chemical lye base. They'd also wear "rags" or cloths or handkerchiefs around it when they slept or played basketball. Do-rags, they were called. But the result was *straight* hair, with a hint of wave. No curl. Do-it-yourselfers took their chances at home with a concoction of mashed potatoes and lye.

The most famous process, outside of what Malcolm X describes   31
in his *Autobiography* and maybe that of Sammy Davis, Jr., was Nat King Cole's. Nat King Cole had patent-leather hair.

"That man's got the finest process money can buy." That's what 32
Daddy said the night Cole's TV show aired on NBC, November 5,
1956. I remember the date because everyone came to our house to
watch it and to celebrate one of Daddy's buddies' birthdays. Yeah,
Uncle Joe chimed in, they can do shit to his hair that the average
Negro can't even *think* about—secret shit.

Nat King Cole was *clean*. I've had an ongoing argument with a 33
Nigerian friend about Nat King Cole for twenty years now. Not
whether or not he could sing; any fool knows that he could sing. But
whether or not he was a handkerchief-head for wearing that patent-
leather process.

Sammy Davis's process I detested. It didn't look good on him. 34
Worse still, he liked to have a fried strand dangling down the middle
of his forehead, shaking it out from the crown when he sang. But Nat
King Cole's hair was a thing unto itself, a beautifully sculpted work
of art that he and he alone should have had the right to wear.

The only difference between a process and a stocking cap, really, 35
was taste; yet Nat King Cole—unlike, say, Michael Jackson—looked
good in his process. His head looked like Rudolph Valentino's in the
twenties, and some say it was Valentino that the process imitated. But
Nat King Cole wore a process because it suited his face, his
demeanor, his name, his style. He was as clean as he wanted to be.

I had forgotten all about Nat King Cole and that patent-leather 36
look until the day in 1971 when I was sitting in an Arab restaurant on
the island of Zanzibar, surrounded by men in fezzes and white caf-
tans, trying to learn how to eat curried goat and rice with the fingers
of my right hand, feeling two million miles from home, when all of a
sudden the old transistor radio sitting on top of a china cupboard
stopped blaring out its Swahili music to play "Fly Me to the Moon"
by Nat King Cole. The restaurant's din was not affected at all, not
even by half a decibel. But in my mind's eye, I saw it: the King's sleek
black magnificent tiara. I managed, barely, to blink back the tears.

ONCE MORE TO THE LAKE

E. B. White

One summer, along about 1904, my father rented a camp on a 1
lake in Maine and took us all there for the month of August. We all
got ringworm from some kittens and had to rub Pond's Extract on
our arms and legs night and morning, and my father rolled over in a
canoe with all his clothes on; but outside of that the vacation was a
success and from then on none of us ever thought there was any
place in the world like that lake in Maine. We returned summer after
summer—always on August 1st for one month. I have since become
a salt-water man, but sometimes in summer there are days when the
restlessness of the tides and the fearful cold of the sea water and the
incessant wind that blows across the afternoon and into the evening
make me wish for the placidity of a lake in the woods. A few weeks
ago this feeling got so strong I bought myself a couple of bass hooks
and a spinner and returned to the lake where we used to go, for a
week's fishing and to revisit old haunts.

I took along my son, who had never had any fresh water up his 2
nose and who had seen lily pads only from train windows. On the
journey over to the lake I began to wonder what it would be like. I
wondered how time would have marred this unique, this holy spot—
the coves and streams, the hills that the sun set behind, the camps and
the paths behind the camps. I was sure that the tarred road would
have found it out and I wondered in what other ways it would be des-
olated. It is strange how much you can remember about places like
that once you allow your mind to return into the grooves that lead
back. You remember one thing, and that suddenly reminds you of
another thing. I guess I remembered clearest of all the early mornings,
when the lake was cool and motionless, remembered how the bedroom smelled of the lumber it was made of and the wet woods whose
scent entered through the screen. The partitions in the camp were thin
and did not extend clear to the top of the rooms, and as I was always
the first up I would dress softly so as not to wake the others, and
sneak out into the sweet outdoors and start out in the canoe, keeping
close along the shore in the long shadows of the pines. I remembered
being very careful never to rub my paddle against the gunwale for
fear of disturbing the stillness of the cathedral.

The lake had never been what you would call a wild lake. There 3
were cottages sprinkled about the shores, and it was in farming coun-

try although the shores of the lake were quite heavily wooded. Some of the cottages were owned by nearby farmers, and you would live at the shore and eat your meals at the farmhouse. That's what our family did. But although it wasn't wild, it was a fairly large and undisturbed lake and there were places in it which, to a child at least, seemed infinitely remote and primeval.

I was right about the tar: It led to within half a mile of the shore.   4
But when I got back there, with my boy, and we settled into a camp near a farmhouse and into the kind of summertime I had known, I could tell that it was going to be pretty much the same as it had been before—I knew it, lying in bed the first morning, smelling the bedroom, and hearing the boy sneak quietly out and go off along the shore in a boat. I began to sustain the illusion that he was I, and therefore, by simple transposition, that I was my father. This sensation persisted, kept cropping up all the time we were there. It was not an entirely new feeling, but in this setting it grew much stronger. I seemed to be living a dual existence. I would be in the middle of some simple act, I would be picking up a bait box or laying down a table fork, or I would be saying something, and suddenly it would be not I but my father who was saying the words or making the gesture. It gave me a creepy sensation.

We went fishing the first morning. I felt the same damp moss cov-   5
ering the worms in the bait can, and saw the dragonfly alight on the tip of my rod as it hovered a few inches from the surface of the water. It was the arrival of this fly that convinced me beyond any doubt that everything was as it always had been, that the years were a mirage and there had been no years. The small waves were the same, chucking the rowboat under the chin as we fished at anchor, and the boat was the same boat, the same color green and the ribs broken in the same places, and under the floorboards the same fresh-water leavings and debris—the dead hellgrammite, the wisps of moss, the rusty discarded fishhook, the dried blood from yesterday's catch. We stared silently at the tips of our rods, at the dragonflies that came and went. I lowered the tip of mine into the water, tentatively, pensively dislodging the fly, which darted two feet away, poised, darted two feet back, and came to rest again a little farther up the rod. There had been no years between the ducking of this dragonfly and the other one— the one that was part of memory. I looked at the boy, who was silently watching his fly, and it was my hands that held his rod, my eyes watching. I felt dizzy and didn't know which rod I was at the end of.

We caught two bass, hauling them in briskly as though they were   6
mackerel, pulling them over the side of the boat in a businesslike

manner without any landing net, and stunning them with a blow on the back of the head. When we got back for a swim before lunch, the lake was exactly where we had left it, the same number of inches from the dock, and there was only the merest suggestion of a breeze. This seemed an utterly enchanted sea, this lake you could leave to its own devices for a few hours and come back to, and find that it had not stirred, this constant and trustworthy body of water. In the shallows, the dark, watersoaked sticks and twigs, smooth and old, were undulating in clusters on the bottom against the clean ribbed sand, and the track of the mussel was plain. A school of minnows swam by, each minnow with its small individual shadow, doubling the attendance, so clear and sharp in the sunlight. Some of the other campers were in swimming, along the shore, one of them with a cake of soap, and the water felt thin and clear and unsubstantial. Over the years there had been this person with the cake of soap, this cultist, and here he was. There had been no years.

Up to the farmhouse to dinner through the teeming, dusty field, 7 the road under our sneakers was only a two-track road. The middle track was missing, the one with the marks of the hooves and splotches of dried, flaky manure. There had always been three tracks to choose from in choosing which track to walk in; now the choice was narrowed down to two. For a moment I missed terribly the middle alternative. But the way led past the tennis court, and something about the way it lay there in the sun reassured me; the tape had loosened along the backline, the alleys were green with plantains and other weeds, and the net (installed in June and removed in September) sagged in the dry noon, and the whole place steamed with midday heat and hunger and emptiness. There was a choice of pie for dessert, and one was blueberry and one was apple, and the waitresses were the same country girls, there having been no passage of time, only the illusion of it as in a dropped curtain—the waitresses were still fifteen; their hair had been washed, that was the only difference—they had been to the movies and seen the pretty girls with the clean hair.

Summertime, oh summertime, pattern of life indelible, the fade- 8 proof lake, the woods unshatterable, the pasture with the sweetfern and the juniper forever and ever, summer without end; this was the background, and the life along the shore was the design, the cottages with their innocent and tranquil design, their tiny docks with the flagpole and the American flag floating against the white clouds in the blue sky, the little paths over the roots of the trees leading from camp to camp and the paths leading back to the outhouses and the can of lime for sprinkling, and at the souvenir counters at the store the miniature birch-bark canoes and the post cards that showed things looking a little better than they looked. This was the American family at play, escaping the city heat, wondering whether the newcomers in the camp at the head of the cove were "common" or "nice," wondering whether it was true that the people who drove up for Sunday dinner at the farmhouse were turned away because there wasn't enough chicken.

It seemed to me, as I kept remembering all this, that those times 9 and those summers had been infinitely precious and worth saving. There had been jollity and peace and goodness. The arriving (at the beginning of August) had been so big a business in itself, at the railway station the farm wagon drawn up, the first smell of the pine-laden air, the first glimpse of the smiling farmer, and the great importance of the trunks and your father's enormous authority in such matters, and the feel of the wagon under you for the long ten-mile haul, and at the top of the last long hill catching the first view of the lake after eleven months of not seeing this cherished body of water. The shouts and cries of the other campers when they saw you, and the trunks to be unpacked, to give up their rich burden. (Arriving was less exciting nowadays, when you sneaked up in your car and parked it under a tree near the camp and took out the bags and in five minutes it was all over, no fuss, no loud wonderful fuss about trunks.)

Peace and goodness and jollity. The only thing that was wrong 10 now, really, was the sound of the place, an unfamiliar nervous sound of the outboard motors. This was the note that jarred, the one thing that would sometimes break the illusion and set the years moving. In those other summertimes all motors were inboard; and when they were at a little distance, the noise they made was a sedative, an ingredient of summer sleep. They were one-cylinder and two-cylinder engines, and some were make-and-break and some were jump-spark, but they all made a sleepy sound across the lake. The one-lungers throbbed and fluttered, and the twin-cylinder ones purred and purred, and that was a quiet sound too. But now the campers all had outboards. In the daytime, in the hot mornings, these motors made a petulant, irritable sound; at night, in the still evening when the afterglow lit the water, they whined about one's ears like mosquitoes. My boy loved our rented outboard, and his great desire was to achieve singlehanded mastery over it, and authority, and he soon learned the trick of choking it a little (but not too much), and the adjustment of the needle valve. Watching him I would remember the things you could do with the old one-cylinder engines with the heavy flywheel, how you could have it eating out of your hand if you got really close to it spiritually. Motor boats in those days didn't have clutches, and you would make a landing by shutting off the motor at the proper time and coasting in with a dead rudder. But there was a way of reversing them, if you learned the trick, by cutting the switch and putting it on again exactly on the final dying revolution of the flywheel, so that it would kick back against compression and begin reversing. Approaching a dock in a strong following breeze, it was difficult to slow up sufficiently by the ordinary coasting method, and if a boy felt he had complete mastery over his motor, he was tempted to keep it running beyond its time and then reverse it a few feet from the dock. It took a cool nerve, because if you threw the switch a twentieth of a second too soon you could catch the flywheel when it still had speed enough to go up past center, and the boat would leap ahead, charging bull-fashion at the dock.

We had a good week at the camp. The bass were biting well and   11
the sun shone endlessly, day after day. We would be tired at night and lie down in the accumulated heat of the little bedrooms after the long hot day and the breeze would stir almost imperceptibly outside and the smell of the swamp drift in through the rusty screens. Sleep would come easily and in the morning the red squirrel would be on the roof, tapping out his gay routine. I kept remembering everything, lying in bed in the mornings—the small steamboat that had a long rounded stern like the lip of a Ubangi, and how quietly she ran on the moonlight sails, when the older boys played their mandolins and the girls sang and we ate doughnuts dipped in sugar, and how sweet the music was on the water in the shining night, and what it had felt like to think about girls then. After breakfast we would go up to the store and the things were in the same place—the minnows in a bottle, the plugs and spinners disarranged and pawed over by the youngsters from the boys' camp, the Fig Newtons and the Beeman's gum. Outside, the road was tarred and cars stood in front of the store. Inside, all was just as it had always been, except there was more Coca-Cola and not so much Moxie and root beer and birch beer and sarsaparilla. We would walk out with a bottle of pop apiece and sometimes the pop would backfire up our noses and hurt. We explored the streams, quietly, where the turtles slid off the sunny logs and dug their way into the soft bottom; and we lay on the town wharf and fed worms to the tame bass. Everywhere we went I had trouble making out which was I, the one walking at my side, the one walking in my pants.

One afternoon while we were there at that lake a thunderstorm 12
came up. It was like the revival of an old melodrama that I had seen
long ago with childish awe. The second-act climax of the drama of
the electrical disturbance over a lake in America had not changed in
any important respect. This was the big scene, still the big scene. The
whole thing was so familiar, the first feeling of oppression and heat
and a general air around camp of not wanting to go very far away. In
midafternoon (it was all the same) a curious darkening of the sky,
and a lull in everything that had made life tick; and then the way the
boats suddenly swung the other way at their moorings with the coming of a breeze out of the new quarter, and the premonitory rumble.
Then the kettle drum, then the snare, then the bass drum and cym-
bals, then crackling light against the dark, and the gods grinning and
licking their chops in the hills. Afterward the calm, the rain steadily
rustling in the calm lake, the return of light and hope and spirits, and
the campers running out in joy and relief to go swimming in the rain,
their bright cries perpetuating the deathless joke about how they
were getting simply drenched, and the children screaming with
delight at the new sensation of bathing in the rain, and the joke about
getting drenched linking the generations in a strong indestructible
chain. And the comedian who waded in carrying an umbrella.

When the others went swimming my son said he was going in 13
too. He pulled his dripping trunks from the line where they had
hung all through the shower, and wrung them out. Languidly, and
with no thought of going in, I watched him, his hard little body,
skinny and bare, saw him wince slightly as he pulled up around his
vitals the small, soggy, icy garment. As he buckled the swollen belt
suddenly my groin felt the chill of death.

THE WAY TO RAINY MOUNTAIN

N. Scott Momaday

A single knoll rises out of the plain in Oklahoma, north and west 1
of the Wichita Range. For my people, the Kiowas, it is an old landmark, and they gave it the name Rainy Mountain. The hardest
weather in the world is there. Winter brings blizzards, hot tornadic
winds arise in the spring, and in summer the prairie is an anvil's
edge. The grass turns brittle and brown, and it cracks beneath your
feet. There are green belts along the rivers and creeks, linear groves
of hickory and pecan, willow and witch hazel. At a distance in July
or August the steaming foliage seems almost to writhe in fire. Great
green and yellow grasshoppers are everywhere in the tall grass, popping up like corn to sting the flesh, and tortoises crawl about on the
red earth, going nowhere in the plenty of time. Loneliness is an
aspect of the land. All things in the plain are isolate; there is no con-
fusion of objects in the eye, but *one* hill or *one* tree or *one* man. To look
upon that landscape in the early morning, with the sun at your back,
is to lose the sense of proportion. Your imagination comes to life, and
this, you think, is where Creation was begun.

I returned to Rainy Mountain in July. My grandmother had died 2
in the spring, and I wanted to be at her grave. She had lived to be
very old and at last infirm. Her only living daughter was with her
when she died, and I was told that in death her face was that of a
child.

I like to think of her as a child. When she was born, the Kiowas 3
were living the last great moment of their history. For more than a
hundred years they had controlled the open range from the Smoky
Hill River to the Red, from the headwaters of the Canadian to the fork
of the Arkansas and Cimarron. In alliance with the Comanches, they
had ruled the whole of the southern Plains. War was their sacred
business, and they were among the finest horsemen the world has
ever known. But warfare for the Kiowas was preeminently a matter
of disposition rather than of survival, and they never understood the
grim, unrelenting advance of the U.S. Cavalry. When at last, divided
and ill-provisioned, they were driven onto the Staked Plains in the
cold rains of autumn, they fell into panic. In Palo Duro Canyon they
abandoned their crucial stores to pillage and had nothing then but
their lives. In order to save themselves, they surrendered to the soldiers at Fort Sill and were imprisoned in the old stone corral that now

stands as a military museum. My grandmother was spared the humiliation of those high gray walls by eight or ten years, but she must have known from birth the affliction of defeat, the dark brooding of old warriors.

Her name was Aho, and she belonged to the last culture to evolve 4
in North America. Her forebears came down from the high country in western Montana nearly three centuries ago. They were a mountain people, a mysterious tribe of hunters whose language has never been positively classified in any major group. In the late seventeenth century they began a long migration to the south and east. It was a journey toward the dawn, and it led to a golden age. Along the way the Kiowas were befriended by the Crows, who gave them the culture and religion of the Plains. They acquired horses, and their ancient nomadic spirit was suddenly free of the ground. They acquired Taime, the sacred Sun Dance doll, from that moment the object and symbol of their worship, and so shared in the divinity of the sun. Not least, they acquired the sense of destiny, therefore courage and pride. When they entered upon the southern Plains they had been transformed. No longer were they slaves to the simple necessity of survival; they were a lordly and dangerous society of fighters and thieves, hunters and priests of the sun. According to their origin myth, they entered the world through a hollow log. From one point of view, their migration was the fruit of an old prophecy, for indeed they emerged from a sunless world.

Although my grandmother lived out her long life in the shadow 5
of Rainy Mountain, the immense landscape of the continental interior lay like memory in her blood. She could tell of the Crows, whom she had never seen, and of the Black Hills, where she had never been. I wanted to see in reality what she had seen more perfectly in the mind's eye, and traveled fifteen hundred miles to begin my pilgrimage.

Yellowstone, it seemed to me, was the top of the world, a region 6
of deep lakes and dark timber, canyons and waterfalls. But, beautiful as it is, one might have the sense of confinement there. The skyline in all directions is close at hand, the high wall of the woods and deep cleavages of shade. There is a perfect freedom in the mountains, but it belongs to the eagle and the elk, the badger and the bear. The Kiowas reckoned their stature by the distance they could see, and they were bent and blind in the wilderness.

Descending eastward, the highland meadows are a stairway to 7
the plain. In July the inland slope of the Rockies is luxuriant with flax

and buckwheat, stonecrop and larkspur. The earth unfolds and the limit of the land recedes. Clusters of trees, and animals grazing far in the distance, cause the vision to reach away and wonder to build upon the mind. The sun follows a longer course in the day, and the sky is immense beyond all comparison. The great billowing clouds that sail upon it are shadows that move upon the grain like water, dividing light. Farther down, in the land of the Crows and Blackfeet, the plain is yellow. Sweet clover takes hold of the hills and bends upon itself to cover and seal the soil. There the Kiowas paused on their way; they had come to the place where they must change their lives. The sun is at home on the plains. Precisely there does it have the certain character of a god. When the Kiowas came to the land of the Crows, they could see the dark lees of the hills at dawn across the Bighorn River, the profusion of light on the grain shelves, the oldest deity ranging after the solstices. Not yet would they veer southward to the caldron of the land that lay below; they must wean their blood from the northern winter and hold the mountains a while longer in their view. They bore Tai-me in procession to the east.

A dark mist lay over the Black Hills, and the land was like iron. 8 At the top of a ridge I caught sight of Devil's Tower upthrust against the gray sky as if in the birth of time the core of the earth had broken through its crust and the motion of the world was begun. There are things in nature that engender an awful quiet in the heart of man; Devil's Tower is one of them. Two centuries ago, because they could not do otherwise, the Kiowas made a legend at the base of the rock. My grandmother said:

> Eight children were there at play, seven sisters and their 9 brother. Suddenly the boy was struck dumb; he trembled and began to run upon his hands and feet. His fingers became claws, and his body was covered with fur. Directly there was a bear where the boy had been. The sisters were terrified; they ran, and the bear after them. They came to the stump of a great tree, and the tree spoke to them. It bade them climb upon it, and as they did so it began to rise into the air. The bear came to kill them, but they were just beyond its reach. It reared against the tree and scored the bark all around with its claws. The seven sisters were borne into the sky, and they became the stars of the Big Dipper.

From that moment, and so long as the legend lives, the Kiowas 10 have kinsmen in the night sky. Whatever they were in the mountains, they could be no more. However tenuous their well-being, however much they had suffered and would suffer again, they had found a way out of the wilderness.

My grandmother had a reverence for the sun, a holy regard that 11 now is all but gone out of mankind. There was a wariness in her, and an ancient awe. She was a Christian in her later years, but she had come a long way about, and she never forgot her birthright. As a child she had been to the Sun Dances; she had taken part in those annual rites, and by them she had learned the restoration of her people in the presence of Tai-me. She was about seven when the last Kiowa Sun Dance was held in 1887 on the Washita River above Rainy Mountain Creek. The buffalo were gone. In order to consummate the ancient sacrifice—to impale the head of a buffalo bull upon the medicine tree—a delegation of old men journeyed into Texas, there to beg and barter for an animal from the Goodnight herd. She was ten when the Kiowas came together for the last time as a living Sun Dance culture. They could find no buffalo; they had to hang an old hide from the sacred tree. Before the dance could begin, a company of soldiers rode out from Fort Sill under orders to disperse the tribe. Forbidden without cause the essential act of their faith, having seen the wild herds slaughtered and left to rot upon the ground, the Kiowas backed away forever from the medicine tree. That was July 20, 1890, at the great bend of the Washita. My grandmother was there. Without bitterness, and for as long as she lived, she bore a vision of deicide.[1]

Now that I can have her only in memory, I see my grandmother 12 in the several postures that were peculiar to her: standing at the wood stove on a winter morning and turning meat in a great iron skillet; sitting at the south window, bent above her beadwork, and afterwards, when her vision failed, looking down for a long time into the fold of her hands; going out upon a cane, very slowly as she did when the weight of age came upon her; praying. I remember her most often at prayer. She made long, rambling prayers out of suffering and hope, having seen many things. I was never sure that I had the right to hear, so exclusive were they of all mere custom and company. The last time I saw her she prayed standing by the side of her bed at night, naked to the waist, the light of a kerosene lamp moving upon her dark skin. Her long, black hair, always drawn and braided in the day, lay upon her shoulders and against her breasts like a shawl. I do not speak Kiowa, and I never understood her prayers, but

---

[1] The killing of a god.

there was something inherently sad in the sound, some merest hesitation upon the syllables of sorrow. She began in a high and descending pitch, exhausting her breath to silence; then again and again—and always the same intensity of effort, of something that is, and is not, like urgency in the human voice. Transported so in the dancing light among the shadows of her room, she seemed beyond the reach of time. But that was illusion; I think I knew then that I should not see her again.

Houses are like sentinels in the plain, old keepers of the weather 13 watch. There, in a very little while, wood takes on the appearance of great age. All colors wear soon away in the wind and rain, and then the wood is burned gray and the grain appears and the nails turn red with rust. The windowpanes are black and opaque; you imagine there is nothing within, and indeed there are many ghosts, bones given up to the land. They stand here and there against the sky, and you approach them for a longer time than you expect. They belong in the distance; it is their domain.

Once there was a lot of sound in my grandmother's house, a lot 14 of coming and going, feasting and talk. The summers there were full of excitement and reunion. The Kiowas are a summer people; they abide the cold and keep to themselves, but when the season turns and the land becomes warm and vital they cannot hold still; an old love of going returns upon them. The aged visitors who came to my grandmother's house when I was a child were made of lean and leather, and they bore themselves upright. They wore great black hats and bright ample shirts that shook in the wind. They rubbed fat upon their hair and wound their braids with strips of colored cloth. Some of them painted their faces and carried the scars of old and cherished enmities. They were an old council of warlords, come to remind and be reminded of who they were. Their wives and daughters served them well. The women might indulge themselves; gossip was at once the mark and compensation of their servitude. They made loud and elaborate talk among themselves, full of jest and gesture, fright and false alarm. They went abroad in fringed and flowered shawls, bright beadwork and German silver. They were at home in the kitchen, and they prepared meals that were banquets.

There were frequent prayer meetings, and great nocturnal feasts. 15 When I was a child I played with my cousins outside, where the lamplight fell upon the ground and the singing of the old people rose up around us and carried away into the darkness. There were a lot of good things to eat, a lot of laughter and surprise. And afterwards, when the quiet returned, I lay down with my grandmother and could hear the frogs away by the river and feel the motion of the air.

Now there is funeral silence in the rooms, the endless wake of some final word. The walls have closed in upon my grandmother's house. When I returned to it in mourning, I saw for the first time in my life how small it was. It was late at night, and there was a white moon, nearly full. I sat for a long time on the stone steps by the kitchen door. From there I could see out across the land; I could see the long row of trees by the creek, the low light upon the rolling plains, and the stars of the Big Dipper. Once I looked at the moon and caught sight of a strange thing. A cricket had perched upon the handrail, only a few inches away from me. My line of vision was such that the creature filled the moon like a fossil. It had gone there, I thought, to live and die, for there, of all places, was its small definition made whole and eternal. A warm wind rose up and purled[2] like the longing within me. 16

The next morning I awoke at dawn and went out on the dirt road to Rainy Mountain. It was already hot, and the grasshoppers began to fill the air. Still, it was early in the morning, and the birds sang out of the shadows. The long yellow grass on the mountain shone in the bright light, and a scissortail hied above the land. There, where it ought to be, at the end of a long and legendary way, was my grandmother's grave. Here and there on the dark stones were ancestral names. Looking back once, I saw the mountain and came away. 17

---

[2] Flowed; rippled.

3

COMPARISON/CONTRAST

SEX, LIES, AND CONVERSATION
Deborah Tannen

I was addressing a small gathering in a suburban Virginia living 1
room—a women's group that had invited men to join them.
Throughout the evening, one man had been particularly talkative,
frequently offering ideas and anecdotes, while his wife sat silently
beside him on the couch. Toward the end of the evening, I commented that women frequently complain that their husbands don't
talk to them. This man quickly concurred. He gestured toward his
wife and said, "She's the talker in our family." The room burst into
laughter; the man looked puzzled and hurt. "It's true," he explained.
"When I come home from work I have nothing to say. If she didn't
keep the conversation going, we'd spend the whole evening in
silence."

This episode crystallizes the irony that although American men 2
tend to talk more than women in public situations, they often talk
less at home. And this pattern is wreaking havoc with marriage.

The pattern was observed by political scientist Andrew Hacker 3
in the late '70s. Sociologist Catherine Kohler Riessman reports in her
new book *Divorce Talk* that most of the women she interviewed—but
only a few of the men—gave lack of communication as the reason for
their divorces. Given the current divorce rate of nearly 50 percent,
that amounts to millions of cases in the United States every year—a
virtual epidemic of failed conversation.

In my own research, complaints from women about their hus- 4
bands most often focused not on tangible inequities such as having
given up the chance for a career to accompany a husband to his, or
doing far more than their share of daily life-support work like clean-

ing, cooking, social arrangements and errands. Instead, they focused on communication: "He doesn't listen to me," "He doesn't talk to me." I found, as Hacker observed years before, that most wives want their husbands to be, first and foremost, conversational partners, but few husbands share this expectation of their wives.

In short, the image that best represents the current crisis is the 5
stereotypical cartoon scene of a man sitting at the breakfast table with a newspaper held up in front of his face, while a woman glares at the back of it, wanting to talk.

Linguistic Battle of the Sexes

How can women and men have such different impressions of 6
communication in marriage? Why the widespread imbalance in their interests and expectations?

In the April issue of *American Psychologist*, Stanford University's 7
Eleanor Maccoby reports the results of her own and other's research showing that children's development is most influenced by the social structure of peer interactions. Boys and girls tend to play with children of their own gender, and their sex-separate groups have different organizational structures and interactive norms.

I believe these systematic differences in childhood socialization 8
make talk between women and men like cross-cultural communication, heir to all the attraction and pitfalls of that enticing but difficult enterprise. My research on men's and women's conversations uncovered patterns similar to those described for children's groups.

For women, as for girls, intimacy is the fabric of relationships, 9
and talk is the thread from which it is woven. Little girls create and maintain friendships by exchanging secrets; similarly, women regard conversation as the cornerstone of friendship. So a woman expects her husband to be a new and improved version of a best friend. What is important is not the individual subjects that are discussed but a sense of closeness, of a life shared, that emerges when people tell their thoughts, feelings, and impressions.

Bonds between boys can be as intense as girls', but they are 10
based less on talking, more on doing things together. Since they don't assume talk is the cement that binds a relationship, men don't know what kind of talk women want and they don't miss it when it isn't there.

Boys' groups are larger, more inclusive, and more hierarchical, so 11
boys must struggle to avoid the subordinate position in the group.

This may play a role in women's complaints that men don't listen to them. Some men really don't like to listen, because being the listener makes them feel one-down, like a child listening to adults or an employee to a boss.

But often when women tell men, "You aren't listening," and the men protest, "I am," the men are right. The impression of not listening results from misalignments in the mechanics of conversation. The misalignment begins as soon as a man and a woman take physical positions. This became clear when I studied videotapes made by psychologist Bruce Dorval of children and adults talking to their same-sex best friends. I found that at every age, the girls and women faced each other directly, their eyes anchored on each other's faces. At every age, the boys and men sat at angles to each other and looked elsewhere in the room, periodically glancing at each other. They were obviously attuned to each other, often mirroring each other's movements. But the tendency of men to face away can give women the impression they aren't listening even when they are. A young woman in college was frustrated: Whenever she told her boyfriend she wanted to talk to him, he would lie down on the floor, close his eyes, and put his arm over his face. This signaled to her, "He's taking a nap." But he insisted he was listening extra hard. Normally, he looks around the room, so he is easily distracted. Lying down and covering his eyes helped him concentrate on what she was saying. 12

Analogous to the physical alignment that women and men take in conversation is their topical alignment. The girls in my study tended to talk at length about one topic, but the boys tended to jump from topic to topic. The second-grade girls exchanged stories about people they knew. The second-grade boys teased, told jokes, noticed things in the room and talked about finding games to play. The sixth-grade girls talked about problems with a mutual friend. The sixth-grade boys talked about 55 different topics, none of which extended over more than a few turns. 13

Listening to Body Language

Switching topics is another habit that gives women the impression men aren't listening, especially if they switch to a topic about themselves. But the evidence of the tenth-grade boys in my study indicates otherwise. The tenth-grade boys sprawled across their chairs with bodies parallel and eyes straight ahead, rarely looking at each other. They looked as if they were riding in a car, staring out the 14 windshield. But they were talking about their feelings. One boy was upset because a girl had told him he had a drinking problem, and the other was feeling alienated from all his friends.

Now, when a girl told a friend about a problem, the friend 15 responded by asking probing questions and expressing agreement and understanding. But the boys dismissed each other's problems. Todd assured Richard that his drinking was "no big problem" because "sometimes you're funny when you're off your butt." And when Todd said he felt left out, Richard responded, "Why should you? You know more people than me."

Women perceive such responses as belittling and unsupportive. 16 But the boys seemed satisfied with them. Whereas women reassure each other by implying, "You shouldn't feel bad because I've had similar experiences," men do so by implying, "You shouldn't feel bad because your problems aren't so bad."

There are even simpler reasons for women's impression that men 17 don't listen. Linguist Lynette Hirschman found that women make more listener-noise, such as "mhm," "uhuh," and "yeah," to show "I'm with you." Men, she found, more often give silent attention. Women who expect a stream of listener-noise interpret silent attention as no attention at all.

Women's conversational habits are as frustrating to men as men's 18 are to women. Men who expect silent attention interpret a stream of listener-noise as overreaction or impatience. Also, when women talk to each other in a close, comfortable setting, they often overlap, finish each other's sentences and anticipate what the other is about to say. This practice, which I call "participatory listenership," is often perceived by men as interruption, intrusion and lack of attention.

A parallel difference caused a man to complain about his wife, 19 "She just wants to talk about her own point of view. If I show her another view, she gets mad at me." When most women talk to each other, they assume a conversationalist's job is to express agreement and support. But many men see their conversational duty as pointing out the other side of an argument. This is heard as disloyalty by women, and refusal to offer the requisite support. It is not that women don't want to see other points of view, but that they prefer them phrased as suggestions and inquiries rather than as direct challenges.

In his book *Fighting for Life*, Walter Ong points out that men use 20 "agonistic" or warlike, oppositional formats to do almost anything; thus discussion becomes debate, and conversation a competitive sport. In contrast, women see conversation as a ritual means of establishing rapport. If Jane tells a problem and June says she has a similar one, they walk away feeling closer to each other. But this attempt at establishing rapport can backfire when used with men. Men take too literally women's ritual "troubles talk," just as women mistake men's ritual challenges for real attack.

The Sounds of Silence

These differences begin to clarify why women and men have 21 such different expectations about communication in marriage. For women, talk creates intimacy. Marriage is an orgy of closeness: you can tell your feelings and thoughts, and still be loved. Their greatest fear is being pushed away. But men live in a hierarchical world, where talk maintains independence and status.They are on guard to protect themselves from being put down and pushed around.   22

This explains the paradox of the talkative man who said of his silent wife, "She's the talker." In the public setting of a guest lecture, he felt challenged to show his intelligence and display his understanding of the lecture. But at home, where he has nothing to prove and no one to defend against, he is free to remain silent. For his wife, being home means she is free from the worry that something she says might offend someone, or spark disagreement, or appear to be showing off; at home she is free to talk.

The communication problems that endanger marriage can't be 23 fixed by mechanical engineering. They require a new conceptual framework about the role of talk in human relationships. Many of the psychological explanations that have become second nature may not be helpful, because they tend to blame either women (for not being assertive enough) or men (for not being in touch with their feelings). A sociolinguistic approach by which male-female conversation is seen as cross-cultural communication allows us to understand the problem and forge solutions without blaming either party.

Once the problem is understood, improvement comes naturally, 24 as it did to the young woman and her boyfriend who seemed to go to sleep when she wanted to talk. Previously, she had accused him of not listening, and he had refused to change his behavior, since that would be admitting fault.But then she learned about and explained to him the differences in women's and men's habitual ways of aligning themselves in conversation. The next time she told him she wanted to talk, he began, as usual, by lying down and covering his eyes. When the familiar negative reaction bubbled up, she reassured herself that he really was listening. But then he sat up and looked at her. Thrilled, she asked why. He said, "You like me to look at you when we talk, so I'll try to do it." Once he saw their differences as cross-cultural rather than right and wrong, he independently altered his behavior.

Women who feel abandoned and deprived when their husbands 25 won't listen to or report daily news may be happy to discover their husbands trying to adapt once they understand the place of small talk in women's relationships. But if their husbands don't adapt, the women may still be comforted that for men, this is not a failure of intimacy. Accepting the difference, the wives may look to their friends or family for that kind of talk. And husbands who can't provide it shouldn't feel their wives have made unreasonable demands. Some couples will still decide to divorce, but at least their decisions will be based on realistic expectations.

In these times of resurgent ethnic conflicts, the world desperately 26 needs cross-cultural understanding. Like charity, successful cross-cultural communication should begin at home.

HOW IT FEELS TO BE COLORED ME

Zora Neale Hurston

I am colored but I offer nothing in the way of extenuating circumstances except the fact that I am the only Negro in the United States whose grandfather on the mother's side was *not* an Indian chief.

I remember the very day that I became colored. Up to my thirteenth year I lived in the little Negro town of Eatonville, Florida. It is exclusively a colored town. The only white people I knew passed through the town going to or coming from Orlando. The native whites rode dusty horses, the Northern tourists chugged down the sandy village road in automobiles. The town knew the Southerners and never stopped cane chewing[1] when they passed. But the Northerners were something else again. They were peered at cautiously from behind curtains by the timid. The more venturesome would come out on the porch to watch them go past and got just as much pleasure out of the tourists as the tourists got out of the village.

The front porch might seem a daring place for the rest of the town, but it was a gallery seat for me. My favorite place was atop the gate-post. Proscenium[2] box for a born first-nighter. Not only did I enjoy the show, but I didn't mind the actors knowing that I liked it. I usually spoke to them in passing. I'd wave at them and when they returned my salute, I would say something like this: "Howdy-do-well-I-thank-you- where-you-goin'?" Usually the automobile or the horse paused at this, and after a queer exchange of compliments, I would probably "go a piece of the way" with them, as we say in farthest Florida. If one of my family happened to come to the front in time to see me, of course negotiations would be rudely broken off. But even so, it is clear that I was the first "welcome-to-our-state" Floridian, and I hope the Miami Chamber of Commerce will please take notice.

During this period, white people differed from colored to me only in that they rode through town and never lived there. They liked to hear me "speak pieces" and sing and wanted to see me dance the parse-mela, and gave me generously of their small silver for doing these things, which seemed strange to me for I wanted to do them so

---

[1] Chewing sugar cane.

[2] In the ancient Greek theater, the stage; in the modern theater, the opening that frames the stage area.

much that I needed bribing to stop. Only they didn't know it. The colored people gave no dimes. They deplored any joyful tendencies in me, but I was their Zora nevertheless. I belonged to them, to the nearby hotels, to the county—everybody's Zora.

But changes came in the family when I was thirteen, and I was 5 sent to school in Jacksonville. I left Eatonville, the town of the oleanders,[3] as Zora. When I disembarked from the river-boat at Jacksonville, she was no more. It seemed that I had suffered a sea change. I was not Zora of Orange County any more, I was now a little colored girl. I found it out in certain ways. In my heart as well as in the mirror, became a fast brown—warranted not to rub nor run.

But I am not tragically colored. There is no great sorrow dammed 6 up in my soul, nor lurking behind my eyes. I do not mind at all. I do not belong to the sobbing school of Negrohood who hold that nature somehow has given them a lowdown dirty deal and whose feelings are all hurt about it. Even in the helter-skelter skirmish that is my life, I have seen that the world is to the strong regardless of a little pigmentation more or less. No, I do not weep at the world—I am too busy sharpening my oyster knife.[4]

Someone is always at my elbow reminding me that I am the 7 granddaughter of slaves. It fails to register depression with me. Slavery is sixty years in the past. The operation was successful and the patient is doing well, thank you. The terrible struggle[5] that made me an American out of a potential slave said "On the line!" The Reconstruction[6] said "Get set!"; and the generation before said "Go!" I am off to a flying start and I must not halt in the stretch to look behind and weep. Slavery is the price I paid for civilization, and the choice was not with me. It is a bully adventure and worth all that I have paid through my ancestors for it. No one on earth ever had a greater chance for glory. The world to be won and nothing to be lost. It is thrilling to think—to know that for any act of mine, I shall get twice as much praise or twice as much blame. It is quite exciting to hold the center of the national stage, with the spectators not knowing whether to laugh or to weep.

The position of my white neighbor is much more difficult. No 8 brown specter pulls up a chair beside me when I sit down to eat. No

---

[3] Tropical flowers.
[4] Reference is to the expression "The world is my oyster."
[5] The Civil War.
[6] The period immediately following the Civil War.

dark ghost thrusts its leg against mine in bed. The game of keeping what one has is never so exciting as the game of getting.

I do not always feel colored. Even now I often achieve the uncon- 9 scious Zora of Eatonville before the Hegira.[7] I feel most colored when I am thrown against a sharp white background.

For instance at Barnard. "Beside the waters of the Hudson" I feel 10 my race. Among the thousand white persons, I am a dark rock surged upon, and overswept, but through it all, I remain myself. When covered by the waters, I am; and the ebb but reveals me again.

Sometimes it is the other way around. A white person is set 11 down in our midst, but the contrast is just as sharp for me. For instance, when I sit in the drafty basement that is The New World Cabaret with a white person, my color comes. We enter chatting about any little nothing that we have in common and are seated by the jazz waiters. In the abrupt way that jazz orchestras have, this one plunges into a number. It loses no time in circumlocutions, but gets right down to business. It constricts the thorax and splits the heart with its tempo and narcotic harmonies. This orchestra grows rambunctious, rears on its hind legs and attacks the tonal veil with primitive fury, rending it, clawing it until it breaks through to the jungle beyond. I follow those heathen—follow them exultingly. I dance wildly inside myself; I yell within, I whoop; I shake my assegai[8] above my head, I hurl it true to the mark *yeeeeooww!* I am in the jungle and living in the jungle way. My face is painted red and yellow and my body is painted blue. My pulse is throbbing like a war drum. I want to slaughter something—give paid, give death to what, I do not know. But the piece ends. The men of the orchestra wipe their lips and rest their fingers. I creep back slowly to the veneer we call civilization with the last tone and find the white friend sitting motionless in his seat, smoking calmly.

"Good music they have here," he remarks, drumming the table 12 with his fingertips.

Music. The great blobs of purpose and red emotion have not 13 touched him. He has only heard what I felt. He is far away and I see him but dimly across the ocean and the continent that have fallen between us. He is so pale with his whiteness then and I am so colored.

---

[7] The flight of Muhammad from Mecca in A.D. 622.
[8] South African hunting spear.

At certain times I have no race, I am *me*. When I set my hat at a   14
certain angle and saunter down Seventh Avenue, Harlem City, feeling as snooty as the lions in front of the Forty-Second Street Library,
for instance. So far as my feelings are concerned, Peggy Hopkins
Joyce[9] on the Boule Mich with her gorgeous raiment, stately carriage,
knees knocking together in a most aristocratic manner, has nothing
on me. The cosmic Zora emerges. I belong to no race nor time. I am
the eternal feminine with its string of beads.

I have no separate feeling about being an American citizen and   15
colored. I am merely a fragment of the Great Soul that surges within
the boundaries. My country, right or wrong.

Sometimes, I feel discriminated against, but it does not make me   16
angry. It merely astonishes me. How *can* any deny themselves the
pleasure of my company? It's beyond me.

But in the main, I feel like a brown bag of miscellany propped   17
against a wall. Against a wall in company with other bags, white, red
and yellow. Pour out the contents, and there is discovered a jumble of
small things priceless and worthless. A first-water diamond, an empty
spool, bits of broken glass, lengths of string, a key to a door long since
crumbled away, a rusty knife-blade, old shoes saved for a road that
never was and never will be, a nail bent under the weight of things too
heavy for any nail, a dried flower or two still a little fragrant. In your
hand is the brown bag. On the ground before you is the jumble it
held—so much like the jumble in the bags, could they be emptied, that
all might be dumped in a single heap and the bags refilled without
altering the contents of any greatly. A bit of colored glass more or less
would not matter. Perhaps that is how the Great Stuffer of Bags filled
them in the first place—who knows?

---

[9] American known for setting trends in beauty and fashion in the 1920s. The Boule Mich (also
Boul' Mich), short for *Boulevard St. Michel,* is a street on Paris's Left Bank.

READING THE RIVER

Mark Twain

Now when I had mastered the language of this water and had ₁ come to know every trifling feature that bordered the great river as familiarly as I knew the letters of the alphabet, I had made a valuable acquisition. But I had lost something, too. I had lost something which could never be restored to me while I lived. All the grace, the beauty, the poetry, had gone out of the majestic river! I still kept in mind a certain wonderful sunset which I witnessed when steamboating was new to me. A broad expanse of the river was turned to blood; in the middle distance the red hue brightened into gold, through which a solitary log came floating, black and conspicuous; in one place a long, slanting mark lay sparkling upon the water; in another the surface was broken by boiling, tumbling rings, that were as many-tinted as an opal; where the ruddy flush was faintest, was a smooth spot that was covered with graceful circles and radiating lines, ever so delicately traced; the shore on our left was densely wooded and the somber shadow that fell from this forest was broken in one place by a long, ruffled trail that shone like silver; and high above the forest wall a clean-stemmed dead tree waved a single leafy bough that glowed like a flame in the unobstructed splendor that was flowing from the sun. There were graceful curves, reflected images, woody heights, soft distances, and over the whole scene, far and near, the dissolving lights drifted steadily, enriching it every passing moment with new marvels of coloring.

I stood like one bewitched. I drank it in, in a speechless rapture. ₂ The world was new to me and I had never seen anything like this at home. But as I have said, a day came when I began to cease from noting the glories and the charms which the moon and the sun and the twilight wrought upon the river's face; another day came when I ceased altogether to note them. Then, if that sunset scene had been repeated, I should have looked upon it without rapture, and should have commented upon it inwardly after this fashion: "This sun means that we are going to have wind to-morrow; that floating log means that the river is rising, small thanks to it; that slanting mark on the water refers to a bluff reef which is going to kill somebody's steamboat one of these nights, if it keeps on stretching out like that; those tumbling 'boils' show a dissolving bar and a changing channel there; the lines and circles in the slick water over yonder are a warning that that troublesome place is shoaling up dangerously; that silver streak in the shadow of the forest is the 'break' from a new snag and he has located himself in the very best place he could have found to fish for steamboats; that tall dead tree, with a single living branch, is not going to last long, and then how is a body ever going to get through this blind place at night without the friendly old landmark?"

No, the romance and beauty were all gone from the river. All the value any feature of it had for me now was the amount of usefulness it could furnish toward compassing the safe piloting of a steamboat. Since those days, I have pitied doctors from my heart. What does the lovely flush in a beauty's cheek mean to a doctor but a "break" that ripples above some deadly disease?[1] Are not all her visible charms sown thick with what are to him the signs and symbols of hidden decay? Does he ever see her beauty at all, or doesn't he simply view her professionally and comment upon her unwholesome condition all to himself? And doesn't he sometimes wonder whether he has gained most or lost most by learning his trade?

---

[1] Red cheeks are one of the signs of tuberculosis.

4

PROCESS ANALYSIS

HOW TO WRITE WITH STYLE
Kurt Vonnegut

Newspaper reporters and technical writers are trained to reveal 1 almost nothing about themselves in their writings. This makes them freaks in the world of writers, since almost all of the other ink-stained wretches in that world reveal a lot about themselves to readers. We call these revelations, accidental and intentional, elements of literary style.

These revelations are fascinating to us as readers. They tell us 2 what sort of person it is with whom we are spending time. Does the writer sound ignorant or informed, crazy or sane, stupid or bright, crooked or honest, humorless or playful—? And on and on.

When you yourself put words on paper, remember that the most 3 damning revelation you can make about yourself is that you do not know what is interesting and what is not. Don't you yourself like or dislike writers mainly for what they choose to show you or make you think about? Did you ever admire an empty-headed writer for his or her mastery of the language? No.

So your own winning literary style must begin with interesting 4 ideas in your head. Find a subject you care about and which you in your heart feel others should care about. It is this genuine caring, and not your games with language, which will be the most compelling and seductive element in your style.

I am not urging you to write a novel, by the way—although I 5 would not be sorry if you wrote one, provided you genuinely cared about something. A petition to the mayor about a pothole in front of your house or a love letter to the girl next door will do.

Do not ramble, though.   6

As for your use of language: Remember that two great masters of 7
our language, William Shakespeare and James Joyce, wrote sentences
which were almost childlike when their subjects were most profound. "To be or not to be?" asks Shakespeare's Hamlet. The longest
word is three letters long. Joyce, when he was frisky, could put
together a sentence as intricate and glittering as a necklace for
Cleopatra, but my favorite sentence in his short story "Eveline" is
this one: "She was tired." At that point in the story, no other words
could break the heart of a reader as those words do.

Simplicity of language is not only reputable, but perhaps even 8
sacred. The Bible opens with a sentence well within the writing skills
of a lively fourteen-year-old: "In the beginning God created the heav-
ens and the earth."

It may be that you, too, are capable of making necklaces for 9
Cleopatra, so to speak. But your eloquence should be the servant of
the ideas in your head. Your rule might be this: If a sentence, no matter how excellent, does not illuminate my subject in some new and
useful way, scratch it out. Here is the same rule paraphrased to apply
to storytelling, to fiction: Never include a sentence which does not
either remark on character or advance the action.

The writing style which is most natural for you is bound to echo 10
speech you heard when a child. English was the novelist Joseph
Conrad's third language, and much that seems piquant in his use of
English was no doubt colored by his first language, which was
Polish. And lucky indeed is the writer who has grown up in Ireland,
for the English spoken there is so amusing and musical. I myself
grew up in Indianapolis, Indiana, where common speech sounds like
a band saw cutting galvanized tin and employs a vocabulary as
unornamental as a monkey wrench.

In some of the more remote hollows of Appalachia, children 11
still grow up hearing songs and locutions of Elizabethan times.
Yes, and many Americans grow up hearing a language other than
English, or an English dialect a majority of Americans cannot
understand.   12

All these varieties of speech are beautiful, just as the varieties of
butterflies are beautiful. No matter what your first language, you
should treasure it all your life. If it happens not to be standard
English, and if it shows itself when you write standard English, the
result is usually delightful, like a very pretty girl with one eye that is
green and one that is blue.

I myself find that I trust my own writing most, and others seem 13
to trust it most, too, when I sound most like a person from
Indianapolis, which is what I am. What alternatives do I have? The
one most vehemently recommended by teachers has no doubt been
pressed on you, as well: that I write like cultivated Englishmen of a
century or more ago.

I used to be exasperated by such teachers, but am no more. I 14
understand now that all those antique essays and stories with which
I was to compare my own work were not magnificent for their dated-
ness or foreignness, but for saying precisely what their authors meant
them to say. My teachers wished me to write accurately, always selecting the most effective words, and relating the words to one another
unambiguously, rigidly, like parts of a machine. The teachers did not
want to turn me into an Englishman after all. They hoped that I would
become understandable—and therefore understood.

And there went my dream of doing with words what Pablo 15
Picasso did with paint or what any number of jazz idols did with
music. If I broke all the rules of punctuation, had words mean whatever I wanted them to mean, and strung them together higgledy-pig-
gledy, I would simply not be understood. So you, too, had better
avoid Picasso-style or jazz-style writing, if you have something
worth saying and wish to be understood.

If it were only teachers who insisted that modern writers stay 16
close to literary styles of the past, we might reasonably ignore them.
But readers insist on the very same thing. They want our pages to
look very much like pages they have seen before.

Why? It is because they themselves have a tough job to do, and 17
they need all the help they can get from us. They have to identify
thousands of little marks on paper, and make sense of them immediately. They have to *read*, an art so difficult that most people do not
really master it even after having studied it all through grade school
and high school—for twelve long years.

So this discussion, like all discussions of literary styles, must 18
finally acknowledge that our stylistic options as writers are neither
numerous nor glamorous, since our readers are bound to be such
imperfect artists. Our audience requires us to be sympathetic and
patient teachers, ever willing to simplify and clarify—whereas we
would rather soar high above the crowd, singing like nightingales.

That is the bad news. The good news is that we Americans are 19
governed under a unique Constitution, which allows us to write
whatever we please without fear of punishment. So the most mean-

ingful aspect of our styles, which is what we choose to write about, is unlimited.

Also: We are members of an egalitarian society, so there is no rea- 20 son for us to write, in case we are not classically educated aristocrats, as though we were classically educated aristocrats.

For a discussion of literary style in a narrower sense, in a more 21 technical sense, I commend to your attention *The Elements of Style* by William Strunk, Jr., and E. B. White (Macmillan, 1979). It contains such rules as this: "A participial phrase at the beginning of a sentence must refer to the grammatical subject," and so on. E. B. White is, of course, one of the most admirable literary stylists this country has so far produced.

You should realize, too, that no one would care how well or 22 badly Mr. White expressed himself, if he did not have perfectly enchanting things to say.

E-MAIL: WHAT YOU SHOULD—AND SHOULDN'T—SAY

Mark Hansen

Most e-mail users remember to check the spelling in the messages they compose. But they often neglect to check how their communication will come across to their readers. Even well-meaning individuals write messages that they would never say aloud. To ensure that your e-mail does not short-circuit a business relationship, consider these 11 common-sense guidelines. 1

1. Think about who may read your message. You should consider not only the person the message is for, but others who may read it. Consider the possibility that your message will take an unexpected turn and appear in the wrong mailbox. Do you need to comment about a third party in your message? Is what you need to say negative or could it be construed as such? If so, consider using the phone or a face-to-face meeting. 2

2. Picture the recipient's reaction to your message. Would you say the same thing you are writing to this person in a face-to-face conversation? Have you inadvertently been sarcastic or judgmental? Is the recipient someone who might put a negative spin on your message? 3

Remember: in a verbal conversation, you might try to temper the bluntness in your message or the exasperation you feel by using facial expression or tone. But this is difficult to achieve via e-mail, even if you use a smile symbol. Why chance creating anxiety or distrust? 4

3. Avoid beginning with criticism. Don't start a message with "Why didn't you answer me sooner?" Though some procrastinators may deserve such a blunt reminder, you'll do more for any relationship if you open with a positive statement. 5

Example: "I wasn't sure if my message got through yesterday, so here it is again." Electronic messages that begin with "why didn't you" can come across as even more directing and authoritarian than when speaking on the phone or in person. 6

4. Don't send a message that you would be embarrassed 7 to send to a family member. Why risk sending something that has innuendoes or remarks that would offend someone? Apply what I call the "Aunt Alma test." If my prim-and-proper Aunt Alma would not find the remark amusing or appropriate, I scrap it. Save funny remarks and jokes for a face-to-face conversation with an audience you know will be amused.

5. Make sure your message is not too cryptic. Have you clearly 8 stated all the reader needs to know? Or have you withheld certain details so that you retain control and force the recipient to "read between the lines," guess, or assume?

Keep this in mind: Information control is a communication 9 power-play that can easily backfire.

6. Check your messages for grammatical idiosyncrasies. Do 10 you often use ellipses instead of completing your thoughts? Do you get carried away with particular punctuation—e-mail symbols some use in place of words to indicate thoughts and feelings? Some symbols may confuse rather than communicate.

7. Read and reread messages before sending them. Would you 11 be offended by the tone? If your tone is harsh, the recipient may think that s/he has done something to offend you.

8. Make sure your message is concise. Do you consistently 12 write more than necessary? Are you swamping your readers with too many details? Do you give so much information—important, unimportant, and in particular order—that your reader cannot easily conclude what matters and what does not?

A poll published in *Oregon Business* found that 26 percent of 13 respondents spend an hour each day reading and replying to e-mail; 14 percent spent more than an hour. So, do everything possible to compose messages that will help your reader save time. Some guidelines:

- Limit messages to one screen so the reader will not have to scroll down

- Use numbers, bullets, etc., to highlight key points

9. Avoid cluttering others' electronic space with non-urgent 14 items that you could send via fax or regular mail. Do you immediately broadcast every tidbit you come across? Don't assume that those you communicate with are not up to speed on the latest news and trends.

This also falls under the "know your audience" heading. Make it 15 your business to know what information sources they use. If you know they subscribe to magazine X or only service Y, why fire off a message about something you just read there?

10. Don't let e-mail become a substitute for in-person or phone 16 **conversations.** Guard against using e-mail to converse with colleagues in the office next door. Unless the message must be in writing, try communicating the old-fashioned way: face to face. Walk down the hall to speak with colleagues. Invite them to lunch. Use the phone. Often, a phone conversation takes a fraction of the time needed to compose a message, send it, and wait for an answer.

11. Remember the human element in communication. Readers 17 will respond more willingly to the writer who does so. Do you add a personal line when you know the reader well? Do you say thank you? The e-mail medium may be cutting-edge, but it will never replace the old-fashioned "please" and "thank you."

Unless some clever person creates a courtesy checking program, 18 you'll benefit from your own courtesy check. That means you must recognize that the tone of what you write should reflect the type of message you yourself expect to find in your electronic in-box.

How to Say Nothing in Five Hundred Words

Paul Roberts

It's Friday afternoon, and you have almost survived another 1
week of classes. You are just looking forward dreamily to the weekend when the English instructor says: "For Monday you will turn in
a five-hundred-word composition on college football."

Well, that puts a good big hole in the weekend. You don't have 2
any strong views on college football one way or the other. You get
rather excited during the season and go to all the home games and
find it rather more fun than not. On the other hand, the class has been
reading Robert Hutchins in the anthology and perhaps Shaw's
"Eighty-Yard Run," and from the class discussion you have got the
idea that the instructor thinks college football is for the birds. You are
no fool. You can figure out what side to take.

After dinner you get out the portable typewriter that you got for 3
high school graduation. You might as well get it over with and enjoy
Saturday and Sunday. Five hundred words is about two double-
spaced pages with normal margins. You put in a sheet of paper, think
up a title, and you're off:

> Why College Football Should Be Abolished
>
> College football should be abolished because it's bad for the school
> and also bad for the players. The players are so busy practicing that
> they don't have any time for their studies.

This, you feel, is a mighty good start. The only trouble is that it's 4
only thirty-two words. You still have four hundred and sixty-eight to
go, and you've pretty well exhausted the subject. It comes to you that
you do your best thinking in the morning, so you put away the typewriter and go to the movies. But the next morning you have to do
your washing and some math problems, and in the afternoon you go
to the game. The English instructor turns up too, and you wonder if
you've taken the right side after all. Saturday night you have a date,
and Sunday morning you have to go to church. (You can't let English

assignments interfere with your religion.) What with one thing and another, it's ten o'clock Sunday night before you get out the typewriter again. You make a pot of coffee and start to fill out your views on college football. Put a little meat on the bones.

Why College Football Should Be Abolished

In my opinion, it seems to me that college football should be abolished. The reason why I think this to be true is because I feel that football is bad for the colleges in nearly every aspect. As Robert Hutchins says in his article in our anthology in which he discusses college football, it would be better if the colleges had race horses and had races with one another, because then the horses would not have to attend classes. I firmly agree with Mr. Hutchins on this point, and I am sure that many other students would agree too.

One reason why it seems to me that college football is bad is that it has become too commercial. In the olden times when people played football just for the fun of it, maybe college football was all right, but they do not play football just for the fun of it now as they used to in the old days. Nowadays college football is what you might call a big business. Maybe this is not true at all schools, and I don't think it is especially true here at State, but certainly this is the case at most colleges and universities in America nowadays, as Mr. Hutchins points out in his very interesting article. Actually the coaches and alumni go around to the high schools and offer the high school stars large salaries to come to their colleges and play football for them. There was one case where a high school star was offered a convertible if he would play football for a certain college.

Another reason for abolishing college football is that it is bad for the players. They do not have time to get a college education, because they are so busy playing football. A football player has to practice every afternoon from three to six and then he is so tired that he can't concentrate on his studies. He just feels like dropping off to sleep after dinner, and then the next day he goes to his classes without having studied and maybe he fails the test.

(Good ripe stuff so far, but you're still a hundred and fifty-one words from home. One more push.)

Also I think college football is bad for the colleges and the universities because not very many students get to participate in it. Out of a college of ten thousand students only seventy-five or a hundred play football, if that many. Football is what you might call a spectator sport. That means that most people go to watch it but do not play it themselves.

(Four hundred and fifteen. Well, you still have the conclusion, 9 and when you retype it, you can make the margins a little wider.)

These are the reasons why I agree with Mr. Hutchins that college football should be abolished in American colleges and universities.

On Monday you turn it in, moderately hopeful, and on Friday it 10 comes back marked "weak in content" and sporting a big "D."

This essay is exaggerated a little, not much. The English instruc- 11 tor will recognize it as reasonably typical of what an assignment on college football will bring in. He knows that nearly half of the class will contrive in five hundred words to say that college football is too commercial and bad for the players. Most of the other half will inform him that college football builds character and prepares one for life and brings prestige to the school. As he reads paper after paper all saying the same thing in almost the same words, all blood-less, five hundred words dripping out of nothing, he wonders how he allowed himself to get trapped into teaching English when he might have had a happy and interesting life as an electrician or a confidence man.

Well, you may ask, what can you do about it? The subject is one 12 on which you have few convictions and little information. Can you be expected to make a dull subject interesting? As a matter of fact, this is precisely what you are expected to do. This is the writer's essential task. All subjects, except sex, are dull until somebody makes them interesting. The writer's job is to find the argument, the approach, the angle, the wording that will take the reader with him. This is seldom easy, and it is particularly hard in subjects that have been much discussed: College Football, Fraternities, Popular Music, Is Chivalry Dead?, and the like. You will feel that there is nothing you can do with such subjects except repeat the old bromides. But there are some things you can do which will make your papers, if not throbbingly alive, at least less insufferably tedious than they might otherwise be.

Avoid the Obvious Content

Say the assignment is college football. Say that you've decided to 13 be against it. Begin by putting down the arguments that come to your mind: It is too commercial, it takes the students' minds off their studies, it is hard on the players, it makes the university a kind of circus instead of an intellectual center, for most schools it is financially ruinous. Can you think of any more arguments, just off hand? All right. Now when you write your paper, *make sure that you don't use any of the material on this list.* If these are the points that leap to your mind they will leap to everyone else's too, and whether you get a "C" or a "D" may depend on whether the instructor reads your paper early when he is fresh and tolerant or late, when the sentence "In my opinion, college football has become too commercial," inexorably repeated, has brought him to the brink of lunacy.

Be against college football for some reason or reasons of your 14 own. If they are keen and perceptive ones, that's splendid. But even if they are trivial or foolish or indefensible, you are still ahead so long as they are not everybody else's reasons too. Be against it because the colleges don't spend enough money on it to make it worthwhile, because it is bad for the characters of the spectators, because the players are forced to attend classes, because the football stars hog all the beautiful women, because it competes with baseball and is therefore un-American and possibly Communist inspired. There are lots of more or less unused reasons for being against college football.

Sometimes it is a good idea to sum up and dispose of the trite 15 and conventional points before going on to your own. This has the advantage of indicating to the reader that you are going to be neither trite nor conventional. Something like this:

> We are often told that college football should be abolished because it has become too commercial or because it is bad for the players. These arguments are no doubt very cogent, but they don't go to the heart of the matter.

Then you go to the heart of the matter.

Take the Less Usual Side

One rather simple way of getting into your paper is to take the 16 side of the argument that most of the citizens will want to avoid. If the assignment is an essay on dogs, you can, if you choose, explain that dogs are faithful and lovable companions, intelligent, useful as guardians of the house and protectors of children, indispensable in police work—in short, when all is said and done, man's best friends. Or you can suggest that those big brown eyes conceal, more often than not, a vacuity of mind and an inconstancy of purpose; that the dogs you have known most intimately have been mangy, ill-tempered brutes, incapable of instruction; and that only your nobility of mind and fear of arrest prevent you from kicking the flea-ridden animals when you pass them on the street.

Naturally personal convictions will sometimes dictate your 17 approach. If the assigned subject is "Is Methodism Rewarding to the Individual?" and you are a pious Methodist, you have really no choice. But few assigned subjects, if any, will fall in this category. Most of them will lie in broad areas of discussion with much to be said on both sides. They are intellectual exercises, and it is legitimate to argue now one way and now another, as debaters do in similar circumstances. Always take the side that looks to you hardest, least defensible. It will almost always turn out to be easier to write interestingly on that side.

This general advice applies where you have a choice of subjects. 18 If you are to choose among "The Value of Fraternities" and "My Favorite High School Teacher" and "What I Think About Beetles," by all means plump for the beetles. By the time the instructor gets to your paper, he will be up to his ears in tedious tales about the French teacher at Bloombury High and assertions about how fraternities build character and prepare one for life. Your views on beetles, whatever they are, are bound to be a refreshing change.

Don't worry too much about figuring out what the instructor 19 thinks about the subject so that you can cuddle up with him. Chances are his views are no stronger than yours. If he does have convictions and you oppose him, his problem is to keep from grading you higher than you deserve in order to show he is not biased. This doesn't mean that you should always cantankerously dissent from what the instructor says; that gets tiresome too. And if the subject assigned is "My Pet Peeve," do not begin, "My pet peeve is the English instructor who assigns papers on 'my pet peeve.'" This was still funny during the War of 1812, but it has sort of lost its edge since then. It is in general good manners to avoid personalities.

Slip Out of Abstraction

If you will study the essay on college football [near the beginning 20 of this essay], you will perceive that one reason for its appalling dullness is that it never gets down to particulars. It is just a series of not very glittering generalities: "Football is bad for the colleges," "it has become too commercial," "football is a big business," "it is bad for the players," and so on. Such round phrases thudding against the reader's brain are unlikely to convince him, though they may well render him unconscious.

If you want the reader to believe that college football is bad for 21 the players, you have to do more than say so. You have to display the evil. Take your roommate, Alfred Simkins, the second-string center. Picture poor old Alfy coming home from football practice every evening, bruised and aching, agonizingly tired, scarcely able to shovel the mashed potatoes into his mouth. Let us see him stagger-ing up to the room, getting out his econ textbook, peering desper-ately at it with his good eye, falling asleep and failing the test in the morning. Let us share his unbearable tension as Saturday draws near. Will he fail, be demoted, lose his monthly allowance, be forced to return to the coal mines? And if he succeeds, what will be his reward? Perhaps a slight ripple of applause when the third-string center replaces him, a moment of elation in the locker room if the team wins, of despair if it loses. What will he look back on when he grad-uates from college? Toil and torn ligaments. And what will be his future? He is not good enough for pro football, and he is too obscure and weak in econ to succeed in stocks and bonds. College football is tearing the heart from Alfy Simpkins and, when it finishes with him, will callously toss aside the shattered hulk.

This is no doubt a weak enough argument for the abolition of 22 college football, but it is a sight better than saying, in three or four variations, that college football (in your opinion) is bad for players.

Look at the work of any professional writer and notice how con- 23 stantly he is moving from the generality, the abstract statement, to the concrete example, the facts and figures, the illustration. If he is writ-ing on juvenile delinquency, he does not just tell you that juveniles are (it seems to him) delinquent and that (in his opinion) something should be done about it. He shows you juveniles being delinquent, tearing up movie theatres in Buffalo, stabbing high school principals in Dallas, smoking marijuana in Palo Alto. And more than likely he is moving toward some specific remedy, not just a general wringing of the hands.

It is no doubt possible to be *too* concrete, too illustrative or anec- 24 dotal, but few inexperienced writers err this way. For most the soundest advice is to be seeking always for the picture, to be always turning general remarks into seeable examples. Don't say, "Sororities teach girls the social graces." Say, "Sorority life teaches a girl how to carry on a conversation while pouring tea, without sloshing the tea into the saucer." Don't say, "I like certain kinds of popular music very much." Say, "Whenever I hear Gerber Sprinklittle play 'Mississippi Man' on the trombone, my socks creep up my ankles."

Get Rid of Obvious Padding

The student toiling away at his weekly English theme is too often 25 tormented by a figure: five hundred words. How, he asks himself, is he to achieve this staggering total? Obviously by never using one word when he can somehow work in ten.

He is therefore seldom content with a plain statement like "Fast 26 driving is dangerous." This has only four words in it. He takes thought, and the sentence becomes:

> In my opinion, fast driving is dangerous.

Better, but he can do better still:

> In my opinion, fast driving would seem to be rather dangerous.

If he is really adept, it may come out:

> In my humble opinion, though I do not claim to be an expert on this complicated subject, fast driving, in most circumstances, would seem to be rather dangerous in many aspects, or at least so it would seem to me.

Thus four words have been turned into forty, and not an iota of content has been added.

Now this is a way to go about reaching five hundred words, and 27 if you are content with a "D" grade, it is as good a way as any. But if you aim higher, you must work differently. Instead of stuffing your sentences with straw, you must try steadily to get rid of the padding, to make your sentences lean and tough. If you are really working at it, your first draft will greatly exceed the required total, and then you will work it down, thus:

> It is thought in some quarters that fraternities do not contribute as much as might be expected to campus life.

> Some people think that fraternities contribute little to campus life.

The average doctor who practices in small towns or in the country must toil night and day to heal the sick.

Most country doctors work long hours.

When I was a little girl, I suffered from shyness and embarrassment in the presence of others.

I was a shy little girl.

It is absolutely necessary for the person employed as a marine fireman to give the matter of steam pressure his undivided attention at all times.

The fireman has to keep his eye on the steam gauge.

You may ask how you can arrive at five hundred words at this rate. Simple. You dig up more real content. Instead of taking a couple of obvious points off the surface of the topic and then circling warily around them for six paragraphs, you work in and explore, figure out the details. You illustrate. You say that fast driving is dangerous, and then you prove it. How long does it take to stop a car at forty and at eighty? How far can you see at night? What happens when a tire blows? What happens in a head-on collision at fifty miles an hour? Pretty soon your paper will be full of broken glass and blood and headless torsos, and reaching five hundred words will not really be a problem. 28

Call a Fool a Fool

Some of the padding in freshman themes is to be blamed not on anxiety about the word minimum but on excessive timidity. The student writes, "In my opinion, the principal of my high school acted in ways that I believe every unbiased person would have to call foolish." This isn't exactly what he means. What he means is, "My high school principal was a fool." If he was a fool, call him a fool. Hedging the thing about with "in-my-opinion's" and "it-seems-to-me's" and "as-I-see-it's" and "at-least-from-my-point-of-view's" gains you nothing. Delete these phrases whenever they creep into your paper. 29

The student's tendency to hedge stems from a modesty that in other circumstances would be commendable. He is, he realizes, young and inexperienced, and he half suspects that he is dopey and fuzzy-minded beyond the average. Probably only too true. But it 30 doesn't help to announce your incompetence six times in every paragraph. Decide what you want to say and say it as vigorously as possible, without apology and in plain words.

Linguistic diffidence can take various forms. One is what we call 31 *euphemism*. This is the tendency to call a spade "a certain garden implement" or women's underwear "unmentionables." It is stronger in some eras than others and in some people than others, but it always operates more or less in subjects that are touchy or taboo: death, sex, madness, and so on. Thus we shrink from saying "He died last night" but say instead "passed away," "left us," "joined his Maker," "went to his reward." Or we try to take off the tension with a lighter cliché: "kicked the bucket," "cashed in his chips," "handed in his dinner pail." We have found all sorts of ways to avoid saying *mad*: "mentally ill," "touched," "not quite right upstairs," "feeble-minded," "innocent," "simple," "off his trolley," "not in his right mind." Even such a now plain word as *insane* began as a euphemism with the meaning "not healthy."

Modern science, particularly psychology, contributes many poly- 32 syllables in which we can wrap our thoughts and blunt their force. To many writers there is no such thing as a bad schoolboy. Schoolboys are maladjusted or unoriented or misunderstood or in the need of guidance or lacking in continued success toward satisfactory integration of the personality as a social unit, but they are never bad. Psychology no doubt makes us better men and women, more sympathetic and tolerant, but it doesn't make writing any easier. Had Shakespeare been confronted with psychology, "To be or not to be" might have come out, "To continue as a social unit or not to do so. That is the personality problem. Whether 'tis a better sign of integration at the conscious level to display a psychic tolerance toward the maladjustments and repressions induced by one's lack of orientation in one's environment or—" But Hamlet would never have finished the soliloquy.

Writing in the modern world, you cannot altogether avoid mod- 33 ern jargon. Nor, in an effort to get away from euphemism, should you salt your paper with four-letter words. But you can do much if you will mount guard against those roundabout phrases, those echoing polysyllables that tend to slip into your writing to rob it of its crispness and force.

Beware of Pat Expressions

Other things being equal, avoid phrases like "other things being 34 equal." Those sentences that come to you whole, or in two or three doughy lumps, are sure to be bad sentences. They are no creation of yours but pieces of common thought floating in the community soup.

Pat expressions are hard, often impossible, to avoid, because they 35 come too easily to be noticed and seem too necessary to be dispensed with. No writer avoids them altogether, but good writers avoid them more often than poor writers.

By "pat expressions" we mean such tags as "to all practical 36 intents and purposes," "the pure and simple truth," "from where I sit," "the time of his life," "to the ends of the earth," "in the twinkling of an eye," "as sure as you're born," "over my dead body," "under cover of darkness," "took the easy way out," "when all is said and done," "told him time and time again," "parted the best of friends," "stand up and be counted," "gave him the best years of her life," "worked her fingers to the bone." Like other clichés, these expressions were once forceful. Now we should use them only when we can't possibly think of anything else.

Some pat expressions stand like a wall between the writer and 37 thought. Such a one is "the American way of life." Many student writers feel that when they have said that something accords with the American way of life or does not they have exhausted the subject. Actually, they have stopped at the highest level of abstraction. The American way of life is the complicated set of bonds between a hundred and eighty million ways. All of us know this when we think about it, but the tag phrase too often keeps us from thinking about it.

So with many another phrase dear to the politician: "this great 38 land of ours," "the man in the street," "our national heritage." These may prove our patriotism or give a clue to our political beliefs, but otherwise they add nothing to the paper except words.

Colorful Words

The writer builds with words, and no builder uses a raw mater- 39 ial more slippery and elusive and treacherous. A writer's work is a constant struggle to get the right word in the right place, to find that particular word that will convey his meaning exactly, that will persuade the reader or soothe him or startle or amuse him. He never succeeds altogether—sometimes he feels that he scarcely succeeds at all—but such successes as he has are what make the thing worth doing.

There is no book of rules for this game. One progresses through 40 everlasting experiment on the basis of ever-widening experience.

There are few useful generalizations that one can make about words as words, but there are perhaps a few.

Some words are what we call "colorful." By this we mean that they are calculated to produce a picture or induce an emotion. They are dressy instead of plain, specific instead of general, loud instead of soft. Thus, in place of "Her heart beat," we may write, "Her heart *pounded, throbbed, fluttered, danced.*" Instead of "He sat in his chair," we may say, "He *lounged, sprawled, coiled.*" Instead of "It was hot," we may say, "It was *blistering, sultry, muggy, suffocating, steamy, wilting.*" 41

However, it should not be supposed that the fancy word is always better. Often it is as well to write "Her heart beat" or "It was hot" if that is all it did or all it was. Ages differ in how they like their prose. The nineteenth century liked it rich and smoky. The twentieth has usually preferred it lean and cool. The twentieth century writer, like all writers, is forever seeking the exact word, but he is wary of sounding feverish. He tends to pitch it low, to understate it, to throw it away. He knows that if he gets too colorful, the audience is likely to giggle. 42

See how this strikes you: "As the rich, golden glow of the sunset died away along the eternal western hills, Angela's limpid blue eyes looked softly and trustingly into Montague's flashing brown ones, and her heart pounded like a drum in time with the joyous song surging in her soul." Some people like that sort of thing, but most modern readers would say, "Good grief," and turn on the television. 43

Colored Words

Some words we call not so much colorful as colored—that is, loaded with associations, good or bad. All words—except perhaps structure words—have associations of some sort. We have said that the meaning of a word is the sum of the contexts in which it occurs. When we hear a word, we hear with it an echo of all the situations in which we have heard it before. 44

In some words, these echoes are obvious and discussable. The word *mother*, for example, has for most people, agreeable associations. When you hear *mother* you probably think of home, safety, love, food, and various other pleasant things. If one writes, "She was like a mother to me," he gets an effect which he would not get in "She was like an aunt to me." The advertiser makes use of the associations of *mother* by working it in when he talks about his product. The politician works it in when he talks about himself. 45

So also with such words as *home, liberty, fireside, contentment,* 46
patriot, tenderness, sacrifice, childlike, manly, bluff, limpid. All of these
words are loaded with associations that would be rather hard to indicate in a straightforward definition. There is more than a literal difference between "They sat around the fireside" and "They sat around
the stove." They might have been equally warm and happy around
the stove, but *fireside* suggests leisure, grace, quiet tradition, congenial company, and *stove* does not.

Conversely, some words have bad associations. *Mother* suggests 47
pleasant things, but *mother-in-law* does not. Many mothers-in-law are
heroically lovable and some mothers drink gin all day and beat their
children insensible, but these facts of life are beside the point. The
point is that *mother* sounds good and *mother-in-law* does not.

Or consider the word *intellectual.* This would seem to be a com- 48
plimentary term, but in point of fact it is not, for it has picked up
associations of impracticality and ineffectuality and general dopi-
ness. So also such words as *liberal, reactionary, Communist, socialist,
capitalist, radical, schoolteacher, truck driver, undertaker, operator, sales-
man, huckster, speculator.* These convey meaning on the literal level,
but beyond that—sometimes, in some places—they convey contempt
on the part of the speaker.

The question of whether to use loaded words or not depends on 49
what is being written. The scientist, the scholar, try to avoid them; for
the poet, the advertising writer, the public speaker, they are standard
equipment. But every writer should take care that they do not substitute for thought. If you write, "Anyone who thinks that is nothing
but a Socialist (or Communist or capitalist)," you have said nothing
except that you don't like people who think that, and such remarks
are effective only with the most naive readers. It is always a bad mistake to think your readers more naive than they really are.

Colorless Words

But probably most student writers come to grief not with words 50
that are colorful or those that are colored but with those that have no
color at all. A pet example is *nice,* a word we would find it hard to dis-
pense with in casual conversation but which is no longer capable of
adding much to a description. Colorless words are those of such general meaning that in a particular sentence they mean nothing. Slang
adjectives like *cool* ("That's real cool") tend to explode all over the
language. They are applied to everything, lose their original force,
and quickly die.

Beware also of nouns of very general meaning, like *circumstances,* 51
cases, instances, aspects, factors, relationships, attitudes, eventualities, etc.
In most circumstances you will find that those cases of writing which
contain too many instances of words like these will in this and other
aspects have factors leading to unsatisfactory relationships with the
reader resulting in unfavorable attitudes on his part and perhaps
other eventualities, like a grade of "D." Notice also what "etc."
means. It means "I'd like to make this list longer, but I can't think of
any more examples."

5

PERSUASIVE
ARGUMENTATION

SHOULD ENGLISH BE THE LAW?
Robert D. King

We have known race riots, draft riots, labor violence, secession, 1
anti-war protests, and a whiskey rebellion, but one kind of trouble
we've never had: a language riot. Language riot? It sounds like a
joke. The very idea of language as a political force—as something
that might threaten to split a country wide apart—is alien to our way
of thinking and to our cultural traditions.

This may be changing. On August 1 of last year the U.S. House 2
of Representatives approved a bill that would make English the official language of the United States. The vote was 259 to 169, with 223
Republicans and thirty-six Democrats voting in favor and eight
Republicans, 160 Democrats, and one independent voting against.
The debate was intense, acrid, and partisan. On March 25 of last year
the Supreme Court agreed to review a case involving an Arizona law
that would require public employees to conduct government business only in English. Arizona is one of several states that have passed
"Official English" or "English Only" laws. The appeal to the
Supreme Court followed a 6-to-5 ruling, in October of 1995, by a federal appeals court striking down the Arizona law. These events suggest how divisive a public issue language could become in
America—even if it has until now scarcely been taken seriously.

Traditionally, the American way has been to make English the 3
national language—but to do so quietly, locally, without fuss. The
Constitution is silent on language: the Founding Fathers had no need

to legislate that English be the official language of the country. It has always been taken for granted that English *is* the national language, and that one must learn English in order to make it in America.

To say that language has never been a major force in American 4 history or politics, however, is not to say that politicians have always resisted linguistic jingoism. In 1753 Benjamin Franklin voiced his concern that German immigrants were not learning English: "Those [Germans] who come hither are generally the most ignorant Stupid Sort of their own Nation. . . . they will soon so outnumber us, that all the advantages we have will not, in My Opinion, be able to preserve our language, and even our government will become precarious." Theodore Roosevelt articulated the unspoken American linguistic-melting-pot theory when he boomed, "We have room for but one language here, and that is the English language, for we intend to see that the crucible turns our people out as Americans, of American nationality, and not as dwellers in a polyglot boarding house." And: "We must have but one flag. We must also have but one language. That must be the language of the Declaration of Independence, of Washington's Farewell address, of Lincoln's Gettysburg speech and second inaugural."

Official English

TR's linguistic tub-thumping long typified the tradition of 5 American politics. That tradition began to change in the wake of the anything-goes attitudes and the celebration of cultural differences arising in the 1960s. A 1975 amendment to the Voting Rights Act of 1965 mandated the "bilingual ballot" under certain circumstances, notably when the voters of selected language groups reached five percent or more of a voting district. Bilingual education became a byword of educational thinking during the 1960s. By the 1970s linguists had demonstrated convincingly—at least to other academics—that black English (today called African-American vernacular English or Ebonics) was not "bad" English but a different kind of authentic English with its own rules. Predictably, there have been scattered demands that black English be included in bilingual-education programs.

It was against this background that the movement to make 6 English the official language of the country arose. In 1981 Senator S. I. Hayakawa, long a leading critic of bilingual education and bilingual ballots, introduced in the U.S. Senate a constitutional amendment that not only would have made English the official language, but would have prohibited federal and state laws and regulations requiring the use of other languages. His English Language Amendment died in the Ninety-seventh Congress.

In 1983 the organization called U.S. English was founded by 7 Hayakawa and John Tanton, a Michigan ophthalmologist. The primary purpose of the organization was to promote English as the official language of the United States. (The best background readings on America's "neolinguisticism" are the books *Hold Your Tongue*, by James Crawford, and *Language Loyalties*, edited by Crawford, both published in 1992.) Official English initiatives were passed by California in 1986, by Arkansas, Mississippi, North Carolina, North Dakota, and South Carolina in 1987, by Colorado, Florida, and Arizona in 1988, and by Alabama in 1990. The majorities voting for these initiatives were generally not insubstantial: California's, for example, passed by 73 percent.

It was probably inevitable that the Official English (or English 8 Only—the two names are used almost interchangeably) movement would acquire a conservative, almost reactionary undertone in the 1990s. Official English is politically very incorrect. But its cofounder John Tanton brought with him strong liberal credentials. He had been active in the Sierra Club and Planned Parenthood, and in the 1970s served as the national president of Zero Population Growth. Early advisers of U.S. English resist ideological pigeonholing: they included Walter Annenberg, Jacques Barzun, Bruno Bettelheim, Alistair Cooke, Denton Cooley, Walter Cronkite, Angier Biddle Duke, George Gilder, Sidney Hook, Norman Podhoretz, Arnold Schwarzenegger, and Karl Shapiro.[1] In 1987 U.S. English installed as its president Linda Chávez, a Hispanic who had been prominent in the Reagan Administration. A year later she resigned her position, citing "repugnant" and "anti-Hispanic" overtones in an internal memorandum written by Tanton. Tanton, too, resigned, and Walter Cronkite, describing the affair as "embarrassing," left the advisory board. One board member, Norman Cousins, defected in 1986, alluding to the "negative symbolic significance" of California's Official English initiative, Proposition 63. The current chairman of the board and CEO of U.S. English is Mauro E. Mujica, who claims that the organization has 650,000 members.

---

[1] A diverse group of writers, academics, and media figures.

The popular wisdom is that conservatives are pro and liberals 9
con. True, conservatives such as George Will and William F. Buckley
Jr. have written columns supporting Official English. But would anyone characterize as conservatives the present and past U.S. English
board members Alistair Cooke, Walter Cronkite, and Norman
Cousins? One of the strongest opponents of bilingual education is the
Mexican-American writer Richard Rodríguez, best known for his elo-
quent autobiography, *Hunger of Memory* (1982). There is a strain of
American liberalism that defines itself in nostalgic devotion to the
melting pot.

For several years relevant bills awaited consideration in the U.S. 10
House of Representatives. The Emerson Bill (H.R. 123), passed by the
House last August, specifies English as the official language of
government, and requires that the government "preserve and
enhance" the official status of English. Exceptions are made for the
teaching of foreign languages; for actions necessary for public health,
international relations, foreign trade, and the protection of the rights
of criminal defendants; and for the use of "terms of art" from languages other than English. It would, for example, stop the Internal
Revenue Service from sending out income-tax forms and instructions
in languages other than English, but it would not ban the use of foreign languages in census materials or documents dealing with
national security. "*E Pluribus Unum*" can still appear on American
money. U.S. English supports the bill.

What are the chances that some version of Official English will 11
become federal law? Any language bill will face tough odds in the
Senate, because some western senators have opposed English Only
measures in the past for various reasons, among them a desire by
Republicans not to alienate the growing number of Hispanic Republicans, most of whom are uncomfortable with mandated monolingual-
ism. Texas Governor George W. Bush, too, has forthrightly said that he
would oppose any English Only proposals in his state. Several of the
Republican candidates for President in 1996 (an interesting exception
is Phil Gramm) endorsed versions of Official English, as has Newt
Gingrich. While governor of Arkansas, Bill Clinton signed into law an
English Only bill. As President, he has described his earlier action as a
mistake.

Many issues intersect in the controversy over Official English: 12
immigration (above all), the rights of minorities (Spanish-speaking
minorities in particular), the pros and cons of bilingual education
tolerance, how best to educate the children of immigrants, and the
place of cultural diversity in school curricula and in American soci-

ety in general. The question that lies at the root of most of the uneasiness is this: Is America threatened by the preservation of languages other than English? Will America, if it continues on its traditional path of benign linguistic neglect, go the way of Belgium, Canada, and Sri Lanka—three countries among many whose unity is gravely imperiled by language and ethnic conflicts?

Language and Nationality

Language and nationalism were not always so intimately inter- 13 twined. Never in the heyday of rule by sovereign was it a condition of employment that the King be able to speak the language of his subjects. George I spoke no English and spent much of his time away from England, attempting to use the power of his kingship to shore up his German possessions. In the Middle Ages nationalism was not even part of the picture: one owed loyalty to a lord, a prince, a ruler, a family, a tribe, a church, a piece of land, but not to a nation and least of all to a nation as a language unit. The capital city of the Austrian Hapsburg empire was Vienna, its ruler a monarch with effective control of peoples of the most varied and incompatible ethnicities, and languages, throughout Central and Eastern Europe. The official language, and the lingua franca as well, was German. While it stood— and it stood for hundreds of years—the empire was an anachronistic relic of what for most of human history had been the normal relationship between country and language: none.

The marriage of language and nationalism goes back at least to 14 Romanticism and specifically to Rousseau,[2] who argued in his *Essay on the Origin of Languages* that language must develop before politics is possible and that language originally distinguished nations from one another. A little-remembered aim of the French Revolution— itself the legacy of Rousseau—was to impose a national language on France, where regional languages such as Provençal, Breton, and Basque were still strong competitors against standard French, the French of the Ile de France. As late as 1789, when the Revolution began, half the population of the south of France, which spoke Provençal, did not understand French. A century earlier the playwright Racine said that he had had to resort to Spanish and Italian to

---

[2] Jean-Jacques Rousseau (1712–1788), Swiss-French philosopher, novelist, and political theorist, who argued that humans in their natural state are good but are corrupted by society.

make himself understood in the southern French town of Uzès. After the Revolution nationhood itself became aligned with language.

In 1846 Jacob Grimm, one of the Brothers Grimm of fairy-tale 15 fame but better known in the linguistic establishment as a forerunner of modern comparative and historical linguists, said that "a nation is the totality of people who speak the same language." After mid-century, language was invoked more than any other single criterion to define nationality. Language as a political force helped to bring about the unification of Italy and of Germany and the secession of Norway from its union with Sweden in 1905. Arnold Toynbee observed—unhappily—soon after the First World War that "the growing consciousness of Nationality had attached itself neither to traditional frontiers nor to new geographical associations but almost exclusively to mother tongues."

The crowning triumph of the new desideratum was the Treaty 16 of Versailles, in 1919, when the allied victors of the First World War began redrawing the map of Central and Eastern Europe according to nationality as best they could. The magic word was "self-determination," and none of Woodrow Wilson's Fourteen Points[3] mentioned the word "language" at all. Self-determination was thought of as being related to "nationality," which today we would be more likely to call "ethnicity"; but language was simpler to identify than nationality or ethnicity. When it came to drawing the boundary lines of various countries—Czechoslovakia, Yugoslavia, Romania, Hungary, Albania, Bulgaria, Poland—it was principally language that guided the draftsman's hand. (The main exceptions were Alsace-Lorraine, South Tyrol, and the German-speaking parts of Bohemia and Moravia.) Almost by default language became the defining characteristic of nationality.

And so it remains today. In much of the world, ethnic unity and 17 cultural identification are routinely defined by language. To be Arab is to speak Arabic. Bengali identity is based on language in spite of the division of Bengali-speakers between Hindu India and Muslim Bangladesh. When eastern Pakistan seceded from greater Pakistan in 1971, it named itself Bangladesh: *desa* means "country;" the *bangla* means not the Bengali people or the Bengali territory but the Bengali language.

Scratch most nationalist movements and you find a linguistic 18 grievance. The demands for independence of the Baltic states

---

[3] President Woodrow Wilson formulated a fourteen-point European peace plan at the close of World War I; presented to Congress in 1918, it included a number of recommendations for redrawing the map of Europe.

(Latvia, Lithuania, and Estonia) were intimately bound up with fears for the loss of their respective languages and cultures in a sea of Russianness. In Belgium the war between French and Flemish threatens an already weakly fused country. The present atmosphere of Belgium is dark and anxious, costive; the metaphor of divorce is a staple of private and public discourse. The lines of terrorism in Sri Lanka are drawn between Tamil Hindus and Sinhalese Buddhists— and also between the Tamil and Sinhalese languages. Worship of the French language fortifies the movement for an independent Quebec. Whether a united Canada will survive into the twenty-first century is a question too close to call. Much of the anxiety about language in the United States is probably fueled by the "Quebec problem": unlike Belgium, which is a small European country, or Sri Lanka, which is halfway around the world, Canada is our close neighbor.

Language is a convenient surrogate for nonlinguistic claims that 19 are often awkward to articulate, for they amount to a demand for more political and economic power. Militant Sikhs in India call for a state of their own: Khalistan ("Land of the Pure" in Punjabi). They frequently couch this as a demand for a linguistic state, which has a certain simplicity about it, a clarity of motive—justice, even, because states in India are normally linguistic states. But the Sikh demands blend religion, economics, language, and retribution for sins both punished and unpunished in a country where old sins cast long shadows.

Language is an explosive issue in the countries of the former 20 Soviet Union. The language conflict in Estonia has been especially bitter. Ethnic Russians make up almost a third of Estonia's population, and most of them do not speak or read Estonian, although Russians have lived in Estonia for more than a generation. Estonia has passed legislation requiring knowledge of the Estonian language as a condition of citizenship. Nationalist groups in independent Lithuania sought restrictions on the use of Polish—again, old sins, long shadows.

In 1995 protests erupted in Moldova, formerly the Moldavian 21 Soviet Socialist Republic, over language and the teaching of Moldovan history. Was Moldovan history a part of Romanian history or of Soviet history? Was Moldova's language Romanian? Moldovan—earlier called Moldavian—*is* Romanian, just as American English and British English are both English. But in the days of the Moldavian SSR, Moscow insisted that the two languages were different, and in a piece of linguistic nonsense required Moldavian to be written in the Cyrillic alphabet to strengthen the case that it was not Romanian.

The official language of Yugoslavia was Serbo-Croatian, which 22
was never so much a language as a political accommodation. The
Serbian and Croatian languages are mutually intelligible. Serbian is
written in the Cyrillic alphabet, is identified with the Eastern
Orthodox branch of the Catholic Church, and borrows its high-culture words from the east—from Russian and Old Church Slavic.
Croatian is written in the Roman alphabet, is identified with Roman
Catholicism, and borrows its high-culture words from the west—
from German, for example, and Latin. One of the first things the
newly autonomous Republic of Serbia did, in 1991, was to pass a law
decreeing Serbian in the Cyrillic alphabet the official language of the
country. With Croatia divorced from Serbia, the Croatian and Serbian
languages are diverging more and more. Serbo-Croatian has now
passed into history, a language-museum relic from the brief period
when Serbs and Croats called themselves Yugoslavs and pretended
to like each other.

Slovakia, relieved now of the need to accommodate to Czech 23
cosmopolitan sensibilities, has passed a law making Slovak its official language. (Czech is to Slovak pretty much as Croatian is to
Serbian.) Doctors in state hospitals must speak to patients in Slovak,
even if another language would aid diagnosis and treatment. Some
600,000 Slovaks—more than 10 percent of the population—are ethni-
cally Hungarian. Even staff meetings in Hungarian-language schools
must be in Slovak. (The government dropped a stipulation that
church weddings be conducted in Slovak after heavy opposition
from the Roman Catholic Church.) Language inspectors are told to
weed out "all sins perpetrated on the regular Slovak language."
Tensions between Slovaks and Hungarians, who had been getting
along, have begun to arise.

The twentieth century is ending as it began—with trouble in the 24
Balkans and with nationalist tensions flaring up in other parts of the
globe. (Toward the end of his life Bismarck predicted that "some
damn fool thing in the Balkans" would ignite the next war.)
Language isn't always part of the problem. But it usually is.

Unique Otherness

Is there no hope for language tolerance? Some countries manage 25
to maintain their unity in the face of multilingualism. Examples are

Finland, with a Swedish minority, and a number of African and Southeast Asian countries. Two others could not be more unlike as countries go: Switzerland and India.

German, French, Italian, and Romansh are the languages of 26 Switzerland. The first three can be and are used for official purposes; all four are designated "national" languages. Switzerland is politically almost hyperstable. It has language problems (Romansh is losing ground), but they are not major, and they are never allowed to threaten national unity.

Contrary to public perception, India gets along pretty well with 27 a host of different languages. The Indian constitution officially recognizes nineteen languages, English among them. Hindi is specified in the constitution as the national language of India, but that is a pious post-colonial fiction: outside the Hindi-speaking northern heartland of India, people don't want to learn it. English functions more nearly than Hindi as India's lingua franca.

From 1947, when India obtained its independence from the 28 British, until the 1960s blood ran in the streets and people died because of language. Hindi absolutists wanted to force Hindi on the entire country, which would have split India between north and south and opened up other fracture lines as well. For as long as possible Jawaharlal Nehru, independent India's first Prime Minister, resisted nationalist demands to redraw the capricious state boundaries of British India according to language. By the time he capitulated, the country had gained a precious decade to prove its viability as a union.

Why is it that India preserves its unity with not just two lan- 29 guages to contend with, as Belgium, Canada, and Sri Lanka have, but nineteen? The answer is that India, like Switzerland, has a strong national identity. The two countries share something big and almost mystical that holds each together in a union transcending language. That something I call "unique otherness."

The Swiss have what the political scientist Karl Deutsch called 30 "learned habits, preferences, symbols, memories, and patterns of landholding": customs, cultural traditions, and political institutions that bind them closer to one another than to people of France, Germany, or Italy living just across the border and speaking the same language. There is Switzerland's traditional neutrality, its system of universal military training (the "citizen army"), its consensual allegiance to a strong Swiss franc—and fondue, yodeling, skiing, and mountains. Set against all this, the fact that Switzerland has four languages doesn't even approach the threshold of becoming a threat.

As for India, what Vincent Smith, in the *Oxford History of India*, 31 calls its "deep underlying fundamental unity" resides in institutions and beliefs such as caste, cow worship, sacred places, and much more. Consider *dharma, karma,* and *maya,* the three root convictions of Hinduism; India's historical epics; Gandhi; *ahimsa* (nonviolence); vegetarianism; a distinctive cuisine and way of eating; marriage customs; a shared past; and what the Indologist Ainslie Embree calls "Brahmanical ideology."[4] In other words, "We are Indian; we are different."

Belgium and Canada have never managed to forge a stable 32 national identity; Czechoslovakia and Yugoslavia never did either. Unique otherness immunizes countries against linguistic destabilization. Even Switzerland and especially India have problems; in any country with as many different languages as India has, language will never *not* be a problem. However, it is one thing to have a major illness with a bleak prognosis; it is another to have a condition that is irritating and occasionally painful but not life-threatening.

History teaches a plain lesson about language and governments: 33 there is almost nothing the government of a free country can do to change language usage and practice significantly, to force its citizens to use certain languages in preference to others, and to discourage people from speaking a language they wish to continue to speak (The rebirth of Hebrew in Palestine and Israel's successful mandate that Hebrew be spoken and written by Israelis is a unique event in the annals of language history.) Quebec has since the 1970s passed an array of laws giving French a virtual monopoly in the province. One consequence—unintended, one wishes to believe—of these laws is that last year kosher products imported for Passover were kept off the shelves, because the packages were not labeled in French. Wise governments keep their hands off language to the extent that it is politically possible to do so.

We like to believe that to pass a law is to change behavior; but 34 passing laws about language, in a free society, almost never changes attitudes or behavior. Gaelic (Irish) is living out a slow, inexorable decline in Ireland despite enormous government support of every possible kind since Ireland gained its independence from Britain. The

---

[4] *Brahman* refers to a Hindu of the highest caste.

Welsh language, in contrast, is alive today in Wales in spite of heavy discrimination during its history. Three out of four people in the northern and western counties of Gwynedd and Dyfed speak Welsh.

I said earlier that language is a convenient surrogate for other 35 national problems. Official English obviously has a lot to do with concern about immigration, perhaps especially Hispanic immigration. America may be threatened by immigration; I don't know. But America is not threatened by language.

The usual arguments made by academics against Official English 36 are commonsensical. Who needs a law when, according to the 1990 census, 94 percent of American residents speak English anyway? (Mauro E. Mujica, the chairman of U.S. English, cites a higher figure: 97 percent.) Not many of today's immigrants will see their first language survive into the second generation. This is in fact the common lament of first-generation immigrants: their children are not learning their language and are losing the culture of their parents. Spanish is hardly a threat to English, in spite of isolated (and easily visible) cases such as Miami, New York City, and pockets of the Southwest and southern California. The everyday language of south Texas is Spanish, and yet south Texas is not about to secede from America.

But empirical, calm arguments don't engage the real issue: 37 language is a symbol, an icon. Nobody who favors a constitutional ban against flag burning will ever be persuaded by the argument that the flag is, after all, just a "piece of cloth." A draft card in the 1960s, was never merely a piece of paper. Neither is a marriage license.

Language, as one linguist has said, is "not primarily a means of 38 communication but a means of communion." Romanticism exalted language, made it mystical, sublime—a bond of national identity. At the same time, Romanticism created a monster: it made of language a means for destroying a country.

America has that unique otherness of which I spoke. In spite of 39 all our racial divisions and economic unfairness, we have the frontier tradition, respect for the individual, and opportunity; we have our love affair with the automobile; we have in our history a civil war that freed the slaves and was fought with valor; and we have sports, hot dogs, hamburgers, and milk shakes—things big and small, noble and petty, important and trifling. "We are Americans; we are different."

If I'm wrong, then the great American experiment will fail—not 40 because of language but because it no longer means anything to be an American; because we have forfeited that "willingness of the heart" that F. Scott Fitzgerald[5] wrote was America; because we are no longer joined by Lincoln's "mystic chords of memory."

We are not even close to the danger point. I suggest that we relax 41 and luxuriate in our linguistic richness and our traditional tolerance of language differences. Language does not threaten American unity. Benign neglect is a good policy for any country when it comes to language, and it's a good policy for America.

---

[5] Twentieth-century American writer.

THE ETHICS OF EUTHANASIA

Lawrence J. Schneiderman

Should physicians be permitted to offer death among their therapeutic options? Should they be licensed to kill—not inadvertently or negligently but willfully, openly, and compassionately? This, on the most superficial level, is the euthanasia debate. 1

In California, a petition to put this matter before the voters failed to gain sufficient signatures. Perhaps this was because too many of those life-affirming hedonists cringed at the thought of signing their own death warrants, or—more likely in this land where almost everything has a price—because the sponsoring Hemlock Society[1] did not hire enough solicitors. 2

In any case, euthanasia is being performed. 3

As a medical ethicist, when I give talks on this subject to physicians, I always ask: "How many of you have ever hastened death to alleviate the suffering of your patients?" Many hands are raised—uneasily; I can offer them no legal immunity. Of all the humane acts physicians perform, euthanasia is the one we do most furtively. 4

But this is an old story. In 1537, while serving in the army of Francis I, the troubled surgeon Ambroise Paré confided in his diary: 5

> We thronged into the city and passed over the dead bodies and some that were not yet dead, hearing them cry under the feet of our horses, which made a great pity in my heart, and truly I repented that I had gone forth from Paris to see so pitiful a spectacle. Being in the city, I entered a stable, thinking to lodge my horse and that of my man, where I found four dead soldiers and three who were propped against the wall, their faces wholly disfigured, and they neither saw, nor heard, nor spoke, and their clothes yet flaming from the gun powder, which had burnt them. Beholding them with pity there came an old soldier who asked me if there was any means of curing them. I told him no. At once he approached them and cut their throats gently and without anger. Seeing this great cruelty I said to him that he was an evil man. He answered me that he prayed God that when he should be in such a case, he might find someone that would do the same for him, to the end that he might not languish miserably.

---

[1] Organization devoted to the individual's right to suicide.

Today, the euthanasia debate takes place under the shadow of 6
Nazi doctors who appropriated the term to describe the "special
treatment" given first to the physically and mentally handicapped,
then to the weak and elderly, and, finally, to Jews, gypsies, and other
"undesirables" as part of the Final Solution—all in the name of social
hygiene. In that monstrous orgy of evil, numbers replaced names,
bodies replaced souls; all were hauled by the trainload to work or to
death, then converted to ashes or merely dumped in such profusion
that the very earth bubbled. That was no *euthanasia*—no easy, pleasant death. That was ugly, debasing death.

But we are different, are we not? Not like *them*. And yet, and 7
yet . . . didn't we American physicians commit atrocities of our own,
such as allowing untreated blacks to succumb to the "natural course"
of syphilis; misleading Spanish-speaking women into thinking they
were obtaining contraceptives, when in fact they were receiving inac-
tive dummy tablets to distinguish drug side-effects, resulting in
unwanted pregnancies; and injecting cancer cells into unwitting
elderly patients? All for the sake of medical progress . . . we can only
look back and shake our heads.

Worthy colleagues—with whom I respectfully disagree—are so 8
fearful of the "Naziness" in us all that they oppose withholding life-
sustaining treatment from *anyone*: the malformed newborn with no
hope of survival, the permanently unconscious patient, the terminal
cancer patient who begs to be allowed to die. Who would be next?
they argue. The physically and mentally handicapped? The weak
and the elderly? And then? And then? This, of course, is the familiar
"slippery slope" argument. Start with one exception and you
inevitably skid down the moral slope of ever more exceptions. This
also is the euthanasia debate, on a deeper level. What will become of
a society that permits—indeed promotes—death as a social good?

An ethics consultation is where we ponder such questions at the 9
bedside of a patient who perhaps is hopelessly ill. Not infrequently,
back in the doctor's conference room, a harried resident will burst
out: *"What good is it for us to keep him alive anyway?"* I don't regard this
as a callous question for the simple reason that it is phrased intimately and in the singular: Why do *we* keep *him* alive? In contrast,
you'd be surprised how often decent people who possess the most
humane and compassionate sensibilities demand: "Why do *they* keep
them alive?" That question, in my view, is morally indistinguishable
from: "Why do *they* let *them* die?"

For, you see, the first question arises from *this* patient, this spe- 10
cial case, *here*. The second question arises from a state of mind—those

people. *There*. It is a state of mind that provides a dehumanizing abstraction appealing to both extremes of the political spectrum, and it has been applied to both ends of life. It can lead to the demand that *all* handicapped newborns be kept alive without regard to their specific agonies and that life-prolonging treatment be denied to *all* the elderly beyond a certain age.

What is so special about the special case? For those of us in medicine, it exerts a palpable moral power; the special case is our daily news, our gossip, a shaping force in our culture. Case studies and case reports are basic teaching tools. *Case* (from *casus*, "happening," "accident") in its original meaning refers to a unique person in unique circumstances. Physicians are molded by their particular autobiography of cases, by their own singular distressing experiences. My first physical diagnosis teacher said, "Make sure you examine the neck veins. Always. Once I missed a patient with congestive heart failure because I neglected to do so." Since then, I have heard many such honest confessions—covertly, for in the litigious world of contemporary medicine, it is almost treachery to reveal that this is how we learn best, by being wrong. To help my compulsively driven and terrified students get on with their duties, I tell them that, if it is true you learn from your mistakes, someday I will know everything.

And we do learn from our special cases, one by one—sometimes badly and incompletely, but each time the lesson is so painful that ultimately we do learn. For example, as a medical student, I was monitoring the blood pressure of a man dying of acute pulmonary edema and myocardial infarction.[2] The end of a gala evening for him. Next to me was the man's wife—coiffed and elegantly gowned, cradling his head and crooning her love while the man blanched into death. It was a good death, since his physician, who was controlling the intravenous infusion on the other side of the bed, had made sure that the man was heavily sedated with morphine. It was a lesson I took with me to my internship, when I treated my first patient with terminal cancer of the bowel. She was tough, this woman, crusty, white-haired, and quite prepared to die. The searing looks she leveled at me made me very much aware of my youth, my health, my innocence.

Alas, she was right about my innocence. I had not yet learned everything there was to know about morphine. Pumping in large doses to control her pain, I failed to deal with its paralytic effects on the intestine. As a result, her last day was a horror of acute intestinal

11

12

13

---

[2] In layperson's terms, a severe heart attack.

obstruction. I shall never forget the curses she hurled at me between squalls of sewage. I doubt there was a soul in the world who knew or cared that she died, but, of course, she was for me immemorial, a special case. Am I forgiven now that countless others have received the blessing of her curses?—for you can be sure that I never fail to teach the importance of keeping the bowels open when caring for a cancer patient. Am I forgiven? I do not know.

Yet, you can see how easy it is to corrupt this experience, to slide 14 from the special case to a state of mind based upon dehumanizing abstractions. For it was a failure in mechanics that led to the poor woman's suffering, and it is merely with the hope of better attending to such mechanics that we have developed the powerful technology that now pervades medicine. Now we can better manage not only the bowels but also the hearts, livers, kidneys, lungs, and all combinations thereof. How do we know we manage them better? We do randomized, double-blind, prospective experimental trials in which patients are aggregated into treatment groups, outcomes are analyzed, and their differences compared by statistics—another state of mind (a related word, in fact), another set of abstractions. Bearing the weight of these massive studies like armies of pharaonic slaves, we plod step by step up federally funded pyramids of therapeutic progress. Read any good medical journal: It is filled with multiauthored, multi-institutional papers. Modern medicine; how dehumanizing, we are told.

And lo and behold, we are repelled into an opposite state of mind, 15 a sentimental longing to escape such cold-blooded modernity. We applaud the hit play *Whose Life Is It Anyway?*, which ends with the quadriplegic hero rejecting life-sustaining technology and going home to die. As the lights come up, we are left to assume that offstage he will effervesce nobly, wittily, free of hunger, thirst, and embarrassing bodily products—fulfilling Milan Kundera's[3] definition of *kitsch*.

But the facts are not so vaporous, and the truth is not so clean- 16 shaven. For the truth is: Death is not an artist many of us admire. This artist's work is often messy. Pretending otherwise is sentimentality— a state of mind that we define as reaching sentiments too cheaply and easily. Of course, there is also the opposite state of mind, the reaction to sentimentality: cynicism, which can also be arrived at too cheaply

---

[3] Czech novelist and essayist. *Kitsch* is anything that appeals to popular or middlebrow taste.

and easily. Both of these states of mind are false. It is against both of these states of mind that the special case protests.

This, I submit, is what the euthanasia debate is about: theoretical 17 and statistical abstractions versus the anguishing, messy particulars of the special case. In illness, we are made exquisitely aware of what it means to be ourselves, no other, alone—this is happening to me. Those of us still healthy, if we are compassionate, acknowledge and even honor the unbreachable solitude of those who are ill. It joins us in a *community* of human feeling—notice that I do not use the word *state*. Because it is truly human, such a community—unlike the totalitarian state (of politics or of mind)—is as varied and unpredictable as the beings within it. And so, the argument goes, if we honor our fellow human beings—their variety, each and every life—it follows that we must honor how each person chooses to live that life, so long as it causes no harm to others. We must also honor—if fate so grants— whatever coda[4] each person sees fit to put on that life. In euthanasia, as in abortion, this issue of choice gets lost in the rhetorical smoke. No one is really *pro*-abortion. Similarly, no one claims to like euthanasia. Proponents merely want to have these options available in desperate circumstances.

But what will happen then? my worthy colleagues ask. Will 18 things fall apart? Is Nazi Germany our malign destiny? Or could it be, rather, that peaceable kingdom, the Netherlands, where an estimated five to ten thousand patients are administered euthanasia on request (and illegally) every year? Explicitly defined violations simply are not prosecuted. The physician is permitted to administer painless death only when a fully informed, rational patient voluntarily and repeatedly requests it in a medical situation that is considered intolerable and hopeless and unresponsive to any other means of medical relief. As a further safeguard, two physicians must concur with a patient's request. At no time are social goals considered. Each patient is treated as a special case, and in each case the act is voluntary.

But is it necessary to kill? my worthy colleagues argue, dubious 19 that a person in such extremity is capable of any voluntary act and drawing a distinction between "active" and "passive" euthanasia. Can't we simply allow such a case to die? Such a distinction, in my view, makes no sense, now that medicine has become so powerful that almost *any* life can be prolonged, however briefly. And once a decision is made that death is preferable to existence, *any* choice—

---

[4] Concluding section of a musical or dramatic work.

whether giving or withholding treatment, whether it be surgery or antibiotics or narcotics—is an act toward or against that end. So, the only relevant moral questions become *why* (the motive) and *how* (the method). One can have the cruelest motive and employ the kindest method; for example, slipping Gramps an overdose of sleeping medicine to get rid of him and get at his money. Or, one can have the kindest motive and employ the cruelest method: letting him "languish miserably" (in the words of Paré) out of a loving reluctance to hasten his death. Neither of these acts is as morally defensible, in my opinion, as the bloody dagger-thrust performed "gently and without anger" by that old unknown soldier.

And so, while the cautious Dutch carry on, several states— including California, once again—are preparing euthanasia initiatives.[5] And the difficult questions will have to be faced. Can we be both merciful and just in matters of medically administered death? How? Do we keep the laws the way they are and grant no exceptions, thus publicly condemning (while at the same time insidiously perpetuating) unsupervised euthanasia? Or should we change the laws? And if we do so, can we craft them in such a way so as not to destroy hallowed and fragile values? Should we explicitly define and sanction certain acts of humane suicide assisted by physicians? Should we allow patients direct legal access to the necessary drugs? Or should we not attempt to change the laws but only openly acknowledge (as in the Netherlands) certain permissible violations—thus cautioning physicians to weigh each act as one they may have to defend in criminal court? The approach we take will reveal much about ourselves as a society. Are our moral cousins the Nazis or the Dutch? Can we keep our anguish fresh each time we contemplate the end of a fellow human being? Or will our anguish grow stale, allowing us to slide down the slope from "easy death" to "useful death," heaping *them* into nameless, faceless piles, saying there go *they*, not *I*, and discovering too late—as others have before—that if yesterday *they* were the retarded, the handicapped, the Jews, the blacks; and if today *they* are the elderly, the AIDS patient; then tomorrow *they* will be ourselves, wondering where all the others are—common waste requiring special treatment rather than special cases sharing a common fate.

20

---

[5] In late 1997, doctor-assisted suicide became legal in Oregon.

SEX, LIES, AND ADVERTISING

Gloria Steinem

About three years ago, as *glasnost*[1] was beginning and *Ms.* seemed to be ending, I was invited to a press lunch for a Soviet official. He entertained us with anecdotes about new problems of democracy in his country. Local Communist leaders were being criticized in their media for the first time, he explained, and they were angry.

"So I'll have to ask my American friends," he finished pointedly, "how more *subtly* to control the press." In the silence that followed, I said, "Advertising."

The reporters laughed, but later, one of them took me aside: How *dare* I suggest that freedom of the press was limited? How dare I imply that his newsweekly could be influenced by ads?

I explained that I was thinking of advertising's media-wide influence on most of what we read. Even newsmagazines use "soft" cover stories to sell ads, confuse readers with "advertorials," and occasionally self-censor on subjects known to be a problem with big advertisers.

But, I also explained, I was thinking especially of women's magazines. There, it isn't just a little content that's devoted to attracting ads, it's almost all of it. That's why advertisers, not readers, have always been the problem for *Ms.* As the only women's magazine that didn't supply what the ad world euphemistically describes as "supportive editorial atmosphere" or "complementary copy" (for instance, articles that praise food/fashion/beauty subjects to "support" and "complement" food/fashion/beauty ads), *Ms.* could never attract enough advertising to break even.

"Oh, *women's* magazines," the journalist said with contempt. "Everybody knows they're catalogs—but who cares? They have nothing to do with journalism."

I can't tell you how many times I've had this argument in 25 years of working for many kinds of publications. Except as money-making machines—"cash cows" as they are so elegantly called in the trade—women's magazines are rarely taken seriously. Though changes being made by women have been called more far-reaching

---

[1] A policy of greater openness and freedom instituted by the Soviet Union's Communist government in the late 1980s.

than the industrial revolution—and though many editors try hard to reflect some of them in the few pages left to them after all the ad-related subjects have been covered—the magazines serving the female half of this country are still far below the journalistic and ethical standards of news and general interest publications. Most depressing of all, this doesn't even rate an exposé.

If *Time* and *Newsweek* had to lavish praise on cars in general and 8 credit General Motors in particular to get GM ads, there would be a scandal—maybe a criminal investigation. When women's magazines from *Seventeen* to *Lear's* praise beauty products in general and credit Revlon in particular to get ads, it's just business as usual.

1

When *Ms.* began, we didn't consider *not* taking ads. The most 9 important reason was keeping the price of a feminist magazine low enough for most women to afford. But the second and almost equal reason was providing a forum where women and advertisers could talk to each other and improve advertising itself. After all, it was (and still is) as potent a source of information in this country as news or TV and movie dramas.

We decided to proceed in two stages. First, we would convince 10 makers of "people products" used by both men and women but advertised mostly to men—cars, credit cards, insurance, sound equipment, financial services, and the like—that their ads should be placed in a women's magazine. Since they were accustomed to the division between editorial and advertising in news and general interest magazines, this would allow our editorial content to be free and diverse. Second, we would add the best ads for whatever traditional "women's products" (clothes, shampoo, fragrance, food, and so on) that surveys showed *Ms.* readers used. But we would ask them to come in *without* the usual quid pro quo of "complementary copy."

We knew the second step might be harder. Food advertisers have 11 always demanded that women's magazines publish recipes and articles on entertaining (preferably ones that name their products) in return for their ads; clothing advertisers expect to be surrounded by fashion spreads (especially ones that credit their designers); and shampoo, fragrance, and beauty products in general usually insist on positive editorial coverage of beauty subjects, plus photo credits besides. That's why women's magazines look the way they do. But if we could break this link between ads and editorial content, then we wanted good ads for "women's products," too.

By playing their part in this unprecedented mix of *all* the things 12 our readers need and use, advertisers also would be rewarded: Ads for products like cars and mutual funds would find a new growth market; the best ads for women's products would no longer be lost in oceans of ads for the same category; and both would have access to a laboratory of smart and caring readers whose response would help create effective ads for other media as well.

I thought then that our main problem would be the imagery in 13 ads themselves. Car-makers were still draping blondes in evening gowns over the hoods like ornaments. Authority figures were almost always male, even in ads for products that only women used. Sadistic, he-man campaigns even won industry praise. For instance, *Advertising Age* had hailed the infamous Silva Thin cigarette theme, "How to Get a Woman's Attention: Ignore Her," as "brilliant." Even in medical journals, tranquilizer ads showed depressed housewives standing beside piles of dirty dishes and promised to get them back to work.

Obviously, *Ms.* would have to avoid such ads and seek out the 14 best ones—but this didn't seem impossible. *The New Yorker* had been selecting ads for aesthetic reasons for years, a practice that only seemed to make advertisers more eager to be in its pages. *Ebony* and *Essence* were asking for ads with positive black images, and though their struggle was hard, they weren't being called unreasonable.

Clearly, what *Ms.* needed was a very special publisher and ad 15 sales staff. I could think of only one woman with experience on the business side of magazines—Patricia Carbine, who recently had become a vice president of *McCall's* as well as its editor in chief—and the reason I knew her name was a good omen. She had been managing editor at *Look* (really *the* editor, but its owner refused to put a female name at the top of his masthead) when I was writing a column there. After I did an early interview with Cesar Chavez, then just emerging as a leader of migrant labor, and the publisher turned it down because he was worried about ads from Sunkist, Pat was the one who intervened. As I learned later, she had told the publisher she would resign if the interview wasn't published. Mainly because *Look* couldn't afford to lose Pat, it *was* published (and the ads from Sunkist never arrived).

Though I barely knew this woman, she had done two things I 16 always remembered: put her job on the line in a way that editors often talk about but rarely do, and been so loyal to her colleagues that she never told me or anyone outside *Look* that she had done so.

Fortunately, Pat did agree to leave *McCall's* and take a huge cut 17
in salary to become publisher of *Ms*. She became responsible for
training and inspiring generations of young women who joined the
Ms. ad sales force, many of whom went on to become "firsts" at the
top of publishing. When *Ms*. first started, however, there were so few
women with experience selling space that Pat and I made the rounds
of ad agencies ourselves. Later, the fact that *Ms*. was asking companies to do business in a different way meant our saleswomen had to
make many times the usual number of calls—first to convince agencies and then client companies besides—and to present endless
amounts of research. I was often asked to do a final ad presentation,
or see some higher decision-maker, or speak to women employees so
executives could see the interest of women they worked with. That's
why I spent more time persuading advertisers than editing or writing for *Ms*. and why I ended up with an unsentimental education in
the seamy underside of publishing that few writers see (and even
fewer magazines can publish).

Let me take you with us through some experiences, just as they 18
happened:

 • Cheered on by early support from Volkswagen and one or two 19
other car companies, we scrape together time and money to put on a
major reception in Detroit. We know U.S. car-makers firmly believe
that women choose the upholstery, not the car, but we are armed with
statistics and reader mail to prove the contrary: A car is an important
purchase for women, one that symbolizes mobility and freedom.

But almost nobody comes. We are left with many pounds of 20
shrimp on the table, and quite a lot of egg on our face. We blame ourselves for not guessing that there would be a baseball pennant
play-off on the same day, but executives go out of their way to
explain they wouldn't have come anyway. Thus begins ten years of
knocking on hostile doors, presenting endless documentation, and
hiring a full-time saleswoman in Detroit; all necessary before *Ms*. gets
any real results.

This long saga has a semihappy ending: foreign and, later, 21
domestic car-makers eventually provided *Ms*. with enough advertising to make cars one of our top sources of ad revenue. Slowly, Detroit
began to take the women's market seriously enough to put car ads in
other women's magazines, too, thus freeing a few pages from the
hothouse of fashion-beauty-food ads.

But long after figures showed a third, even a half, of many car 22
models being bought by women, U.S. makers continued to be
uncomfortable addressing women. Unlike foreign car-makers,

Detroit never quite learned the secret of creating intelligent ads that exclude no one, and then placing them in women's magazines to overcome past exclusion. (*Ms.* readers were so grateful for a routine Honda ad featuring rack and pinion steering, for instance, that they sent fan mail.) Even now, Detroit continues to ask, "Should we make special ads for women?" Perhaps that's why some foreign cars still have a disproportionate share of the U.S. women's market.

• In the Ms. Gazette, we do a brief report on a congressional 23 hearing into chemicals used in hair dyes that are absorbed through the skin and may be carcinogenic. Newspapers report this too, but Clairol, a Bristol-Myers subsidiary that makes dozens of products— a few of which have just begun to advertise in *Ms.*—is outraged. Not at new papers or news magazines, just at us. It's bad enough that Ms. is the only women's magazine refusing to provide the usual "complementary" articles and beauty photos, but to criticize one of their categories— *that* is going too far.

We offer to publish a letter from Clairol telling its side of the 24 story. In an excess of solicitousness, we even put this letter in the Gazette, not in Letters to the Editors where it belongs. Nonetheless— and in spite of surveys that show *Ms.* readers are active women who use more of almost everything Clairol makes than do the readers of any other women's magazine—*Ms.* gets almost none of these ads for the rest of its natural life.

Meanwhile, Clairol changes its hair-coloring formula, apparently 25 in response to the hearings we reported.

• Our saleswomen set out early to attract ads for consumer 26 electronics: sound equipment, calculators, computers, VCRs, and the like. We know that our readers are determined to be included in the technological revolution. We know from reader surveys that *Ms.* readers are buying this stuff in numbers as high as those of magazines like *Playboy*, or "men 18 to 34," the prime targets of the consumer electronics industry. Moreover, unlike traditional women's products that our readers buy but don't need to read articles about, these are subjects they want covered in our pages. There actually *is* a supportive editorial atmosphere.

"But women don't understand technology," say executives at the 27 end of ad presentations. "Maybe not," we respond, "but neither do men—and we all buy it."

"If women *do* buy it," say the decision-makers, "they're asking 28 their husbands and boyfriends what to buy first." We produce letters from *Ms.* readers saying how turned off they are when salesmen say things like "Let me know when your husband can come in."

After several years of this, we get a few ads for compact sound 29 systems. Some of them come from JVC, whose vice president, Harry Elias, is trying to convince his Japanese bosses that there is something called a women's market. At his invitation, I find myself speaking at huge trade shows in Chicago and Las Vegas, trying to persuade JVC dealers that showrooms don't have to be locker rooms where women are made to feel unwelcome. But as it turns out, the shows themselves are part of the problem. In Las Vegas, the only women around the technology displays are seminude models serving champagne. In Chicago, the big attraction is Marilyn Chambers, who followed Linda Lovelace of *Deep Throat* fame as Chuck Traynor's captive and/or employee. VCRs are being demonstrated with her porn videos.

In the end, we get ads for a car stereo now and then, but no 30 VCRs; some IBM personal computers, but no Apple or Japanese ones. We notice that office magazines like *Working Woman* and *Savvy* don't benefit as much as they should from office equipment ads either. In the electronics world, women and technology seem mutually exclusive. It remains a decade behind even Detroit.

• Because we get letters from little girls who love toy trains, and 31 who ask our help in changing ads and box-top photos that feature little boys only, we try to get toy-train ads from Lionel. It turns out that Lionel executives *have* been concerned about little girls. They made a pink train, and were surprised when it didn't sell.

Lionel bows to consumer pressure with a photograph of a boy 32 *and* a girl—but only on some of their boxes. They fear that, if trains are associated with girls, they will be devalued in the minds of boys. Needless to say, *Ms.* gets no train ads, and little girls remain a mostly unexplored market. By 1986, Lionel is put up for sale.

But for different reasons, we haven't had much luck with other 33 kinds of toys either. In spite of many articles on child-rearing; an annual listing of nonsexist, multiracial toys by Letty Cottin Pogrebin; Stories for Free Children, a regular feature also edited by Letty; and other prizewinning features for or about children, we get virtually no toy ads. Generations of *Ms.* saleswomen explain to toy manufacturers that a larger proportion of *Ms.* readers have preschool children than do the readers of other women's magazines, but this industry can't believe feminists have or care about children.

• When *Ms.* begins, the staff decides not to accept ads for femi- 34 nine hygiene sprays or cigarettes: they are damaging and carry no appropriate health warnings. Though we don't think we should tell our readers what to do, we do think we should provide facts so they can decide for themselves. Since the antismoking lobby has been pressing for health warnings on cigarette ads, we decide to take them only as they comply.

Philip Morris is among the first to do so. One of its brands, 35 Virginia Slims, is also sponsoring women's tennis and the first national polls of women's opinions. On the other hand, the Virginia Slims theme, "You've come a long way, baby," has more than a "baby" problem. It makes smoking a symbol of progress for women.

We explain to Philip Morris that this slogan won't do well in our 36 pages, but they are convinced its success with some women means it will work with *all* women. Finally, we agree to publish an ad for a Virginia Slims calendar as a test. The letters from readers are critical—and smart. For instance: Would you show a black man picking cotton, the same man in a Cardin suit, and symbolize the antislavery and civil rights movements by smoking? Of course not. But instead of honoring the test results, the Philip Morris people seem angry to be proven wrong. They take away ads for *all* their many brands.

This costs *Ms.* about $250,000 the first year. After five years, we 37 can no longer keep track. Occasionally, a new set of executives listens to *Ms.* saleswomen, but because we won't take Virginia Slims, not one Philip Morris product returns to our pages for the next 16 years.

Gradually, we also realize our naiveté in thinking we *could* 38 decide against taking cigarette ads. They became a disproportionate support of magazines the moment they were banned on television, and few magazines could compete and survive without them; certainly not *Ms.*, which lacks so many other categories. By the time statistics in the 1980s showed that women's rate of lung cancer was approaching men's, the necessity of taking cigarette ads has become a kind of prison.

• General Mills, Pillsbury, Carnation, Del Monte, Dole, Kraft, 39 Stouffer, Hormel, Nabisco: You name the food giant, we try it. But no matter how desirable the *Ms.* readership, our lack of recipes is lethal.

We explain to them that placing food ads *only* next to recipes asso- 40 ciates food with work. For many women, it is a negative that works *against* the ads. Why not place food ads in diverse media without recipes (thus reaching more men, who are now a third of the shoppers in supermarkets anyway), and leave the recipes to specialty magazines like *Gourmet* (a third of whose readers are also men)?

These arguments elicit interest, but except for an occasional ad 41 for a convenience food, instant coffee, diet drinks, yogurt, or such extras as avocados and almonds, this mainstay of the publishing industry stays closed to us. Period.

• Traditionally, wines and liquors didn't advertise to women: 42
Men were thought to make the brand decisions, even if women did
the buying. But after endless presentations, we begin to make a dent
in this category. Thanks to the unconventional Michel Roux of
Carillon Importers (distributors of Grand Marnier, Absolut Vodka,
and others), who assumes that food and drink have no gender, some
ads are leaving their men's club.

Beermakers are still selling masculinity. It takes *Ms.* fully eight 43
years to get its first beer ad (Michelob). In general, however, liquor ads
are less stereotyped in their imagery—and far less controlling of the
editorial content around them—than are women's products. But given
the underrepresentation of other categories, these very facts tend to
create a disproportionate number of alcohol ads in the pages of *Ms.*
This in turn dismays readers worried about women and alcoholism.

• We hear in 1980 that women in the Soviet Union have been 44
producing feminist *samizdat* (underground, self-published books)
and circulating them throughout the country. As punishment, four of
the leaders have been exiled. Though we are operating on our usual
shoestring, we solicit individual contributions to send Robin Morgan
to interview these women in Vienna.

The result is an exclusive cover story that includes the first news 45
of a populist peace movement against the Afghanistan occupation, a
prediction of *glasnost* to come, and a grassroots, intimate view of
Soviet women's lives. From the popular press to women's studies
courses, the response is great. The story wins a Front Page award.

Nonetheless, this journalistic coup undoes years of efforts to get 46
an ad schedule from Revlon. Why? Because the Soviet women on our
cover *are not wearing makeup.*

• Four years of research and presentations go into convincing 47
airlines that women now make travel choices and business trips.
United, the first airline to advertise in *Ms.*, is so impressed with the
response from our readers that one of its executives appears in a film
for our ad presentations. As usual, good ads get great results.

But we have problems unrelated to such results. For instance: 48
Because American Airlines flight attendants include among their
labor demands the stipulation that they could choose to have their
last names preceded by "Ms." on their name tags—in a long-delayed
revolt against the standard, "I am your pilot, Captain Rothgart, and
this is your flight attendant, Cindy Sue"—American officials seem to
hold the magazine responsible. We get no ads.

There is still a different problem at Eastern. A vice president can- 49
cels subscriptions for thousands of copies on Eastern flights. Why?

Because he is offended by ads for lesbian poetry journals in the *Ms.* Classified. A "family airline," as he explains to me coldly on the phone, has to "draw the line somewhere."

It's obvious that *Ms.* can't exclude lesbians and serve women. 50 We've been trying to make that point ever since our first issue included an article by and about lesbians, and both Suzanne Levine, our managing editor, and I were lectured by such heavy hitters as Ed Kosner, then editor of *Newsweek* (and now of *New York Magazine*), who insisted that *Ms.* should "position" itself *against* lesbians. But our advertisers have paid to reach a guaranteed number of readers, and soliciting new subscriptions to compensate for Eastern would cost $150,000, plus rebating money in the meantime.

Like almost everything ad-related, this presents an elaborate 51 organizing problem. After days of searching for sympathetic members of the Eastern board, Frank Thomas, president of the Ford Foundation, kindly offers to call Roswell Gilpatrick, a director of Eastern. I talk with Mr. Gilpatrick, who calls Frank Borman, then the president of Eastern. Frank Borman calls me to say that his airline is not in the business of censoring magazines: *Ms.* will be returned to Eastern flights.

• Women's access to insurance and credit is vital, but with the 52 exception of Equitable and a few other ad pioneers, such financial services address men. For almost a decade after the Equal Credit Opportunity Act passes in 1974, we try to convince American Express that women are a growth market—but nothing works.

Finally, a former professor of Russian named Jerry Welsh 53 becomes head of marketing. He assumes that women should be cardholders, and persuades his colleagues to feature women in a campaign. Thanks to this 1980s series, the growth rate for female cardholders surpasses that for men.

For this article, I asked Jerry Welsh if he would explain why 54 American Express waited so long. "Sure," he said, "they were afraid of having a 'pink' card."

• Women of color read *Ms.* in disproportionate numbers. This is 55 a source of pride to *Ms.* staffers, who are also more racially representative than the editors of other women's magazines. But this reality is obscured by ads filled with enough white women to make a reader snowblind.

Pat Carbine remembers mostly "astonishment" when she 56 requested African American, Hispanic, Asian, and other diverse images. Marcia Ann Gillespie, a *Ms.* editor who was previously the editor in chief of *Essence*, witnesses ad bias a second time: Having tried for *Essence* to get white advertisers to use black images (Revlon did so eventually, but L'Oréal, Lauder, Chanel, and other companies never did), she sees similar problems getting integrated ads for an integrated magazine. Indeed, the ad world often creates black and Hispanic ads only for black and Hispanic media. In an exact parallel of the fear that marketing a product to women will endanger its appeal to men, the response is usually, "But your [white] readers won't identify."

In fact, those we are able to get—for instance, a Max Factor 57 ad made for *Essence* that Linda Wachner gives us after she becomes president—are praised by white readers, too. But there are pathetically few such images.

• By the end of 1986, production and mailing costs have risen 58 astronomically, ad income is flat, and competition for ads is stiffer than ever. The 60/40 preponderance of edit over ads that we promised to readers becomes 50/50; children's stories, most poetry, and some fiction are casualties of less space; in order to get variety into limited pages, the length (and sometimes the depth) of articles suffers; and, though we do refuse most of the ads that would look like a parody in our pages, we get so worn down that some slip through. Still, readers perform miracles. Though we haven't been able to afford a subscription mailing in two years, they maintain our guaranteed circulation of 450,000.

Nonetheless, media reports on *Ms.* often insist that our unprof- 59 itability must be due to reader disinterest. The myth that advertisers simply follow readers is very strong. Not one reporter notes that other comparable magazines our size (say, *Vanity Fair* or *The Atlantic*) have been losing more money in one year than *Ms.* has lost in 16 years. No matter how much never-to-be-recovered cash is poured into starting a magazine or keeping one going, appearances seem to be all that matter. (Which is why we haven't been able to explain our fragile state in public. Nothing causes ad flight like the smell of nonsuccess.)

My healthy response is anger. My not-so-healthy response is 60 constant worry. Also an obsession with finding one more rescue. There is hardly a night when I don't wake up with sweaty palms and pounding heart, scared that we won't be able to pay the printer or the post office; scared most of all that closing our doors will hurt the women's movement.

Out of chutzpah and desperation, I arrange a lunch with 61 Leonard Lauder, president of Estée Lauder. With the exception of Clinique (the brainchild of Carol Phillips), none of Lauder's hundreds of products has been advertised in *Ms.* A year's schedule of ads for just three or four of them could save us. Indeed, as the scion of a family-owned company whose ad practices are followed by the beauty industry, he is one of the few men who could liberate many pages in all women's magazines just by changing his mind about "complementary copy."

Over a lunch that costs more than we can pay for some articles, I explain the need for his leadership. I also lay out the record of *Ms.*: more literary and journalistic prizes won, more new issues introduced into the mainstream, new writers discovered, and impact on society than any other magazine; more articles that became books, stories that became movies, ideas that became television series, and newly advertised products that became profitable; and, most important for him, a place for his ads to reach women who aren't reachable through any other women's magazine. Indeed, if there is one constant characteristic of the everchanging *Ms.* readership, it is their impact as leaders. Whether it's waiting until later to have first babies, or pioneering PABA as sun protection in cosmetics, *whatever* they are doing today, a third to a half of American women will be doing three to five years from now. It's never failed. 62

But, he says, *Ms.* readers are not *our* women. They're not interested in things like fragrance and blush-on. If they were, *Ms.* would write articles about them. 63

On the contrary, I explain, surveys show they are more likely to buy such things than the readers of, say, *Cosmopolitan* or *Vogue.* They're good customers because they're out in the world enough to need several sets of everything: home, work, purse, travel, gym, and so on. They just don't need to read articles about these things. Would he ask a men's magazine to publish monthly columns on how to shave before he advertised Aramis products (his line for men)? 64

He concedes that beauty features are often concocted more for advertisers than readers. But *Ms.* isn't appropriate for his ads anyway, he explains. Why? Because Estée Lauder is selling "a kept-woman mentality." 65

I can't quite believe this. Sixty percent of the users of his products are salaried, and generally resemble *Ms.* readers. Besides, his company has the appeal of having been started by a creative and hardworking woman, his mother, Estée Lauder. 66

That doesn't matter, he says. He knows his customers, and they would *like* to be kept women. That's why he will never advertise in *Ms.* 67

In November 1987, by vote of the Ms. Foundation for Education 68
and Communication (*Ms.*'s owner and publisher, the media subsidiary of the Ms. Foundation for Women), *Ms.* was sold to a company whose officers, Australian feminists Sandra Yates and Anne
Summers, raised the investment money in their country that *Ms.*
couldn't find in its own. They also started *Sassy* for teenage women.

In their two-year tenure, circulation was raised to 550,000 by 69
investment in circulation mailings, and, to the dismay of some readers, editorial features on clothes and new products made a more traditional bid for ads. Nonetheless, ad pages fell below previous levels.
In addition, *Sassy*, whose fresh voice and sexual frankness were an
unprecedented success with young readers, was targeted by two
mothers from Indiana who began, as one of them put it, "calling every
Christian organization I could think of." In response to this controversy, several crucial advertisers pulled out.

Such links between ads and editorial content was a problem in 70
Australia, too, but to a lesser degree. "Our readers pay two times
more for their magazines," Anne explained, "so advertisers have less
power to threaten a magazine's viability."

"I was shocked," said Sandra Yates with characteristic directness. 71
"In Australia, we think you have freedom of the press—but you
don't."

Since Anne and Sandra had not met their budget's projections for 72
ad revenue, their investors forced a sale. In October 1989, *Ms.* and
Sassy were bought by Dale Lang, owner of *Working Mother, Working
Woman,* and one of the few independent publishing companies left
among the conglomerates. In response to a request from the original
Ms. staff—as well as to reader letters urging that *Ms.* continue, plus
his own belief that *Ms.* would benefit his other magazines by blazing
a trail—he agreed to try the ad-free, reader-supported *Ms.* . . . and to
give us complete editorial control.

2

In response to the workplace revolution of the 1970s, traditional 73
women's magazines—that is, "trade books" for women working at
home—were joined by *Savvy, Working Woman,* and other trade books
for women working in offices. But by keeping the fashion/beauty/
entertaining articles necessary to get traditional ads and then adding
career articles besides, they inadvertently produced the antifeminist
stereotype of Super Woman. The male-imitative, dress-for-success

woman carrying a briefcase became the media image of a woman worker, even though a blue-collar woman's salary was often higher than her glorified secretarial sister's, and though women at a real briefcase level are statistically rare. Needless to say, these dress-for-success women were also thin, white, and beautiful.

In recent years, advertisers' control over the editorial content of women's magazines has become so institutionalized that it is written into "insertion orders" or dictated to ad salespeople as official policy. The following are recent typical orders to women's magazines: [74]

• Dow's Cleaning Products stipulates that ads for its Vivid and Spray 'n Wash products should be adjacent to "children or fashion editorial"; ads for Bathroom Cleaner should be next to "home furnishing/family" features; and so on for other brands. "If a magazine fails for half the brands or more," the Dow order warns, "it will be omitted from further consideration." [75]

• Bristol-Myers, the parent of Clairol, Windex, Drano, Bufferin, and much more, stipulates that ads be placed next to "a full page of compatible editorial." [76]

• S. C. Johnson & Son, makers of Johnson Wax, lawn and laundry products, insect sprays, hair sprays, and so on, orders that its ads *"should not be opposite extremely controversial features or material antithetical to the nature/copy of the advertised product."* (Italics theirs.) [77]

• Maidenform, manufacturer of bras and other apparel, leaves a blank for the particular product and states: "The creative concept of the _____ campaign, and the very nature of the product itself appeal to the positive emotions of the reader/consumer. Therefore, it is imperative that all editorial agencies reflect that same positive tone. The editorial must not be negative in content or lend itself contrary to the _____ product imagery/message (*e.g., editorial relating to illness, disillusionment, large size fashion, etc.*)." (Italics mine.) [78]

• The De Beers diamond company, a big seller of engagement rings, prohibits magazines from placing its ads with "agencies to hard news or anti- love/romance themed editorial." [79]

• Procter & Gamble, one of this country's most powerful and diversified advertisers, stands out in the memory of Anne Summers and Sandra Yates (no mean feat in this context): Its products were not to be placed in any issue that included *any* material on gun control, abortion, the occult, cults, or the disparagement of religion. Caution was also demanded in any issue covering sex or drugs, even for educational purposes. [80]

Those are the most obvious chains around women's magazines. There are also rules so clear they needn't be written down: for [81] instance, an overall "look" compatible with beauty and fashion ads. Even "real" nonmodel women photographed for a woman's magazine are usually made up, dressed in credited clothes, and retouched out of all reality. When editors do include articles on less-than-cheerful subjects (for instance, domestic violence), they tend to keep them short and unillustrated. The point is to be "upbeat." Just as women in the street are asked, "Why don't you smile, honey?" women's magazines acquire an institutional smile.

Within the text itself, praise for advertisers' products has become 82 so ritualized that fields like "beauty writing" have been invented. One of its frequent practitioners explained seriously that "It's a difficult art. How many new adjectives can you find? How much greater can you make a lipstick sound? The FDA[2] restricts what companies can say on labels, but we create illusion. And ad agencies are on the phone all the time pushing you to get their product in. A lot of them keep the business based on how many editorial clippings they produce every month. The worst are products," like Lauder's as the writer confirmed, "with their own name involved. It's all ego."

Often, editorial becomes one giant ad. Last November, for 83 instance, *Lear's* featured an elegant woman executive on the cover. On the contents page, we learned she was wearing Guerlain makeup and Samsara, a new fragrance by Guerlain. Inside were full-page ads for Samsara and Guerlain antiwrinkle cream. In the cover profile, we learned that this executive was responsible for launching Samsara and is Guerlain's director of public relations. When the *Columbia Journalism Review* did one of the few articles to include women's magazines in coverage of the influence of ads, editor Frances Lear was quoted as defending her magazine because "this kind of thing is done all the time."

Often, advertisers also plunge odd-shaped ads into the text, no 84 matter what the cost to the readers. At *Woman's Day*, a magazine originally founded by a supermarket chain, editor in chief Ellen Levine said, "The day the copy had to rag around a chicken leg was not a happy one."

Advertisers are also adamant about where in a magazine their 85 ads appear. When Revlon was not placed as the first beauty ad in one Hearst magazine, for instance, Revlon pulled its ads from *all* Hearst magazines. Ruth Whitney, editor in chief of *Glamour*, attributes some of these demands to "ad agencies wanting to prove to a client that

---

[2] The federal Food and Drug Administration.

they've squeezed the last drop of blood out of a magazine." She also
is, she says, "sick and tired of hearing that women's magazines are
controlled by cigarette ads." Relatively speaking, she's right. To be as
censoring as are many advertisers for women's products, tobacco
companies would have to demand articles in praise of smoking and
expect glamorous photos of beautiful women smoking their brands.

I don't mean to imply that the editors I quote here share my 86
objections to ads: Most assume that women's magazines have to be the
way they are. But it's also true that only former editors can be completely honest. "Most of the pressure came in the form of direct product mentions," explains Sey Chassler, who was editor in chief of
Redbook from the sixties to the eighties. "We got threats from the big
guys, the Revlons, blackmail threats. They wouldn't run ads unless we
credited them.

"But it's not fair to single out the beauty advertisers because 87
these pressures came from everybody. Advertisers want to know two
things: What are you going to charge me? What *else* are you going to
do for me? It's a holdup. For instance, management felt that fiction
took up too much space. They couldn't put any advertising in that.
For the last ten years, the number of fiction entries into the National
Magazine Awards has declined.

"And pressures are getting worse. More magazines are more 88
bottom-line oriented because they have been taken over by companies with no interest in publishing.

"I also think advertisers do this to women's magazines espe- 89
cially," he concluded, "because of the general disrespect they have
for women."

Even media experts who don't give a damn about women's mag- 90
azines are alarmed by the spread of this ad-edit linkage. In a climate
The Wall Street Journal describes as an unacknowledged Depression
for media, women's products are increasingly able to take their low
standards wherever they go. For instance: Newsweeklies publish
uncritical stories on fashion and fitness. *The New York Times Magazine*
recently ran an article on "firming creams," complete with mentions
of advertisers. Vanity Fair published a profile of one major advertiser,
Ralph Lauren, illustrated by the same photographer who does his
ads, and turned the lifestyle of another, Calvin Klein, into a cover
story. Even the outrageous *Spy* has toned down since it began to go
after fashion ads.

And just to make us really worry, films and books, the last media 91
that go directly to the public without having to attract ads first, are in

danger, too. Producers are beginning to depend on payments for displaying products in movies, and books are now being commissioned by companies like Federal Express.

But the truth is that women's products—like women's maga- 92 zines—have never been the subjects of much serious reporting anyway. News and general interest publications, including the "style" or "living" sections of newspapers, write about food and clothing as cooking and fashion, and almost never evaluate such products by brand name. Though chemical additives, pesticides, and animal fats are major health risks in the United States, and clothes, shoddy or not, absorb more consumer dollars than cars, this lack of information is serious. So is ignoring the contents of beauty products that are absorbed into our bodies through our skins, and that have profit margins so big they would make a loan shark blush.

3

What could women's magazines be like if they were as free as 93 books? as realistic as newspapers? as creative as films? as diverse as women's lives? We don't know.

But we'll only find out if we take women's magazines seriously. 94 If readers were to act in a concerted way to change traditional practices of *all* women's magazines and the marketing of *all* women's products, we could do it. After all, they are operating on our consumer dollars; money that we now control. You and I could:

- write to editors and publishers (with copies to advertisers) that 95 we're willing to pay *more* for magazines with editorial independence, but will *not* continue to pay for those that are just editorial extensions of ads;

- write to advertisers (with copies to editors and publishers) that 96 we want fiction, political reporting, consumer reporting— whatever is, or is not, supported by their ads;

- put as much energy into breaking advertising's control over 97 content as into changing the images in ads, or protesting ads for harmful products like cigarettes;

- support only those women's magazines and products that take 98 *us* seriously as readers and consumers.

- Those of us in the magazine world can also use the carrot-   99
and-stick technique. For instance: Pointing out that, if magazines were a regulated medium like television, the demands of
advertisers would be against FCC[3] rules. Payola and extortion
could be punished. As it is, there are probably illegalities. A
magazine's postal rates are determined by the ratio of ad to edit
pages, and the former costs more than the latter. So much for
the stick.

The carrot means appealing to enlightened self-interest. For   100
instance: There are many studies showing that the greatest factor in
determining an ad's effectiveness is the credibility of its surround-
ings. The "higher the rating of editorial believability," concluded a
1987 survey by the *Journal of Advertising Research*, "the higher the rating of the advertising." Thus, an impenetrable wall between edit and
ads would also be in the best interest of advertisers.

Unfortunately, few agencies or clients hear such arguments.   101
Editors often maintain the false purity of refusing to talk to them at
all. Instead, they see ad salespeople who know little about editorial,
are trained in business as usual, and are usually paid by commission.
Editors might also band together to take on controversy. That happened once when all the major women's magazines did articles in the
same month on the Equal Rights Amendment. It could happen again.

It's almost three years away from life between the grindstones of   102
advertising pressures and readers' needs. I'm just beginning to realize how edges got smoothed down—in spite of all our resistance.

I remember feeling put upon when I changed "Porsche" to "car"   103
in a piece about Nazi imagery in German pornography by Andrea
Dworkin—feeling sure Andrea would understand that Volkswagen,
the distributor of Porsche and one of our few supportive advertisers,
asked only to be far away from Nazi subjects. It's taken me all this
time to realize that Andrea was the one with a right to feel put upon.

Even as I write this, I get a call from a writer for *Elle*, who is doing   104
a whole article on where women part their hair. Why, she wants to
know, do I part mine in the middle?

It's all so familiar. A writer trying to make something of a noth-   105
ing assignment; an editor laboring to think of new ways to attract

---

[3] The Federal Communications Commission.

6

CLASSIFICATION/DIVISION

DOUBLESPEAK

William Lutz

There are no potholes in the streets of Tucson, Arizona, just 1
"pavement deficiencies." The Reagan Administration didn't propose
any new taxes, just "revenue enhancement" through new "user's
fees." Those aren't bums on the street, just "nongoal oriented members of society." There are no more poor people, just "fiscal under-
achievers." There was no robbery of an automatic teller machine, just
an "unauthorized withdrawal." The patient didn't die because of
medical malpractice, it was just a "diagnostic misadventure of a high
magnitude." The U.S. Army doesn't kill the enemy anymore, it just
"services the target." And the doublespeak goes on.

Doublespeak is language that pretends to communicate but 2
really doesn't. It is language that makes the bad seem good, the negative appear positive, the unpleasant appear attractive or at least tol-
erable. Doublespeak is language that avoids or shifts responsibility,
language that is at variance with its real or purported meaning. It is
language that conceals or prevents thought; rather than extending
thought, doublespeak limits it.

Doublespeak is not a matter of subjects and verbs agreeing; it is 3
a matter of words and facts agreeing. Basic to doublespeak is incongruity, the incongruity between what is said or left unsaid, and what
really is. It is the incongruity between the word and the referent,
between seem and be, between the essential function of language—
communication—and what doublespeak does—mislead, distort,
deceive, inflate, circumvent, obfuscate.

How to Spot Doublespeak

How can you spot doublespeak? Most of the time you will rec- 4
ognize doublespeak when you see or hear it. But, if you have any
doubts, you can identify doublespeak just by answering these questions: Who is saying what to whom, under what conditions and circumstances, with what intent, and with what results? Answering
these questions will usually help you identify as doublespeak language that appears to be legitimate or that at first glance doesn't even
appear to be doublespeak.

First Kind of Doublespeak

There are at least four kinds of doublespeak. The first is the 5
euphemism, an inoffensive or positive word or phrase used to avoid
a harsh, unpleasant, or distasteful reality. But a euphemism can also
be a tactful word or phrase which avoids directly mentioning a
painful reality, or it can be an expression used out of concern for the
feelings of someone else, or to avoid directly discussing a topic subject to a social or cultural taboo.

When you use a euphemism because of your sensitivity for 6
someone's feelings or out of concern for a recognized social or cultural taboo, it is not doublespeak. For example, you express your
condolences that someone has "passed away" because you do not
want to say to a grieving person, "I'm sorry your father is dead."
When you use the euphemism "passed away," no one is misled.
Moreover, the euphemism functions here not just to protect the feelings of another person, but to communicate also your concern for
that person's feelings during a period of mourning. When you
excuse yourself to go to the "rest room," or you mention that someone is "sleeping with" or "involved with" someone else, you do not
mislead anyone about your meaning, but you do respect the social
taboos about discussing bodily functions and sex in direct terms. You
also indicate your sensitivity to the feelings of your audience, which
is usually considered a mark of courtesy and good manners.

However, when a euphemism is used to mislead or deceive, 7
it becomes doublespeak. For example, in 1984 the U.S. State
Department announced that it would no longer use the word
"killing" in its annual report on the status of human rights in countries around the world. Instead, it would use the phrase "unlawful or
arbitrary deprivation of life," which the department claimed was
more accurate. Its real purpose for using this phrase was simply to

avoid discussing the embarrassing situation of government-sanctioned killings in countries that are supported by the United States and have been certified by the United States as respecting the human rights of their citizens. This use of a euphemism constitutes doublespeak, since it is designed to mislead, to cover up the unpleasant. Its real intent is at variance with its apparent intent. It is language designed to alter our perception of reality.

The Pentagon, too, avoids discussing unpleasant realities when it refers to bombs and artillery shells that fall on civilian targets as "incontinent ordnance." And in 1977 the Pentagon tried to slip funding for the neutron bomb unnoticed into an appropriations bill by calling it a "radiation enhancement device." 8

Second Kind of Doublespeak

A second kind of doublespeak is jargon, the specialized language of a trade, profession, or similar group, such as that used by doctors, lawyers, engineers, educators, or car mechanics. Jargon can serve an important and useful function. Within a group, jargon functions as a kind of verbal shorthand that allows members of the group to communicate with each other clearly, efficiently, and quickly. Indeed, it is a mark of membership in the group to be able to use and understand the group's jargon. 9

But jargon, like the euphemism, can also be doublespeak. It can be—and often is—pretentious, obscure, and esoteric terminology used to give an air of profundity, authority, and prestige to speakers and their subject matter. Jargon as doublespeak often makes the simple appear complex, the ordinary profound, the obvious insightful. In this sense it is used not to express but impress. With such doublespeak, the act of smelling something becomes "organoleptic analysis," glass becomes "fused silicate," a crack in a metal support beam becomes a "discontinuity," conservative economic policies become "distributionally conservative notions." 10

Lawyers, for example, speak of an "involuntary conversion" of property when discussing the loss or destruction of property through theft, accident, or condemnation. If your house burns down or if your car is stolen, you have suffered an involuntary conversion of your property. When used by lawyers in a legal situation, such jargon is a legitimate use of language, since lawyers can be expected to understand the term. 11

However, when a member of a specialized group uses its jargon to communicate with a person outside the group, and uses it know- 12 ing that the nonmember does not understand such language, then there is doublespeak. For example, on May 9, 1978, a National Airlines 727 airplane crashed while attempting to land at the Pensacola, Florida, airport. Three of the fifty-two passengers aboard the airplane were killed. As a result of the crash, National made an after-tax insurance benefit of $1.7 million, or an extra 18¢ a share dividend for its stockholders. Now National Airlines had two problems: It did not want to talk about one of its airplanes crashing, and it had to account for the $1.7 million when it issued its annual report to its stockholders. National solved the problem by inserting a footnote in its annual report which explained that the $1.7 million income was due to "the involuntary conversion of a 727." National thus acknowledged the crash of its airplane and the subsequent profit it made from the crash, without once mentioning the accident or the deaths. However, because airline officials knew that most stockholders in the company, and indeed most of the general public, were not familiar with legal jargon, the use of such jargon constituted doublespeak.

Third Kind of Doublespeak

A third kind of doublespeak is gobbledygook or bureaucratese. 13 Basically, such doublespeak is simply a matter of piling on words, of overwhelming the audience with words, the bigger the words and the longer the sentences the better. Alan Greenspan, then chair of President Nixon's Council of Economic Advisors, was quoted in the *Philadelphia Inquirer* in 1974 as having testified before a Senate committee that "It is a tricky problem to find the particular calibration in timing that would be appropriate to stem the acceleration in risk premiums created by falling incomes without prematurely aborting the decline in the inflation-generated risk premiums."

Nor has Mr. Greenspan's language changed since then. Speaking 14 to the meeting of the Economic Club of New York in 1988, Mr. Greenspan, now Federal Reserve chair, said, "I guess I should warn you, if I turn out to be particularly clear, you've probably misunderstood what I've said." Mr. Greenspan's doublespeak doesn't seem to have held back his career.

Sometimes gobbledygook may sound impressive, but when the 15 quote is later examined in print it doesn't even make sense. During the 1988 presidential campaign, vice-presidential candidate Senator Dan Quayle explained the need for a strategic defense initiative by saying, "Why wouldn't an enhanced deterrent, a more stable peace, a better prospect to denying the ones who enter conflict in the first place to have a reduction of offensive systems and an introduction to defensive capability? I believe this is the route the country will eventually go."

The investigation into the Challenger disaster in 1986 revealed the doublespeak of gobbledygook and bureaucratese used by too many involved in the shuttle program. When Jesse Moore, NASA's associate administrator, was asked if the performance of the shuttle program had improved with each launch or if it had remained the same, he answered, "I think our performance in terms of the liftoff performance and in terms of the orbital performance, we knew more about the envelope we were operating under, and we have been pretty accurately staying in that. And so I would say the performance has not by design drastically improved. I think we have been able to characterize the performance more as a function of our launch experience as opposed to it improving as a function of time." While this language may appear to be jargon, a close look will reveal that it is really just gobbledygook laced with jargon. But you really have to wonder if Mr. Moore had any idea what he was saying. [16]

Fourth Kind of Doublespeak

The fourth kind of doublespeak is inflated language that is designed to make the ordinary seem extraordinary; to make everyday things seem impressive; to give an air of importance to people, situations, or things that would not normally be considered important; to make the simple seem complex. Often this kind of doublespeak isn't hard to spot, and it is usually pretty funny. While car mechanics may be called "automotive internists," elevator operators members of the "vertical transportation corps," used cars "preowned" or "experienced cars," and black-and-white television sets described as having "non-multicolor capability," you really aren't misled all that much by such language. [17]

However, you may have trouble figuring out that, when Chrysler "initiates a career alternative enhancement program," it is really laying off five thousand workers; or that "negative patient care outcome" means the patient died; or that "rapid oxidation" means a fire in a nuclear power plant. [18]

The doublespeak of inflated language can have serious consequences. In Pentagon doublespeak, "pre-emptive counterattack" means that American forces attacked first; "engaged the enemy on all [19]

sides" means American troops were ambushed; "backloading of aug-
mentation personnel" means a retreat by American troops. In the doublespeak of the military, the 1983 invasion of Grenada was conducted
not by the U.S. Army, Navy, Air Force, and Marines, but by the
"Caribbean Peace Keeping Forces." But then, according to the
Pentagon, it wasn't an invasion, it was a "predawn vertical insertion."

THE MYTH OF THE LATIN WOMAN: I JUST MET A GIRL NAMED MARIA

Judith Ortiz Cofer

On a bus trip to London from Oxford University where I was   1
earning some graduate credits one summer, a young man, obviously
fresh from a pub, spotted me and as if struck by inspiration went
down on his knees in the aisle. With both hands over his heart he
broke into an Irish tenor's rendition of "Maria" from *West Side Story*.[1]
My politely amused fellow passengers gave his lovely voice the
round of gentle applause it deserved. Though I was not quite as
amused, I managed my version of an English smile: no show of teeth,
no extreme contortions of the facial muscles—I was at this time of my
life practicing reserve and cool. Oh, that British control, how I cov-
eted it. But "Maria" had followed me to London, reminding me of a
prime fact of my life: you can leave the island, master the English language, and travel as far as you can, but if you are a Latina, especially
one like me who so obviously belongs to Rita Moreno's[2] gene pool,
the island travels with you.

This is sometimes a very good thing—it may win you that extra   2
minute of someone's attention. But with some people, the same
things can make *you* an island—not a tropical paradise but an
Alcatraz, a place nobody wants to visit. As a Puerto Rican girl living
in the United States[3] and wanting like most children to "belong," I
resented the stereotype that my Hispanic appearance called forth
from many people I met.

Growing up in a large urban center in New Jersey during the   3
1960s, I suffered from what I think of as "cultural schizophrenia."
Our life was designed by my parents as a microcosm of their *casas*[4]
on the island. We spoke in Spanish, ate Puerto Rican food bought at
the *bodega*,[5] and practiced strict Catholicism at a church that allotted

---

[1] A popular Broadway musical, loosely based on *Romeo and Juliet*, about two rival street gangs,
one Anglo and one Puerto Rican, in New York City.

[2] Puerto Rico–born actress who won an Oscar for her role in the 1960 movie version of *West Side
Story*.

[3] Although it is an island, Puerto Rico is part of the United States (it is a self-governing com-
monwealth).

[4] Homes.

[5] Small grocery store.

us a one-hour slot each week for mass, performed in Spanish by a Chinese priest trained as a missionary for Latin America.

As a girl I was kept under strict surveillance by my parents, since 4 my virtue and modesty were, by their cultural equation, the same as their honor. As a teenager I was lectured constantly on how to behave as a proper *senorita*. But it was a conflicting message I received, since the Puerto Rican mothers also encouraged their daughters to look and act like women and to dress in clothes our Anglo friends and their mothers found too "mature" and flashy. The difference was, and is, cultural; yet I often felt humiliated when I appeared at an American friend's party wearing a dress more suitable to a semi-formal than to a playroom birthday celebration. At Puerto Rican festivities, neither the music nor the colors we wore could be too loud.

I remember Career Day in our high school, when teachers told us 5 to come dressed as if for a job interview. It quickly became obvious that to the Puerto Rican girls "dressing up" meant wearing their mother's ornate jewelry and clothing, more appropriate (by mainstream standards) for the company Christmas party than as daily office attire. That morning I had agonized in front of my closet, trying to figure out what a "career girl" would wear. I knew how to dress for school (at the Catholic school I attended, we all wore uniforms), I knew how to dress for Sunday mass, and I knew what dresses to wear for parties at my relatives' homes. Though I do not recall the precise details of my Career Day outfit, it must have been a composite of these choices. But I remember a comment my friend (an Italian American) made in later years that coalesced my impressions of that day. She said that at the business school she was attending, the Puerto Rican girls always stood out for wearing "everything at once." She meant, of course, too much jewelry, too many accessories. On that day at school we were simply made the negative models by the nuns, who were themselves not credible fashion experts to any of us. But it was painfully obvious to me that to the others, in their tailored skirts and silk blouses, we must have seemed "hopeless" and "vulgar." Though I now know that most adolescents feel out of step much of the time, I also know that for the Puerto Rican girls of my generation that sense was intensified. The way our teachers and classmates looked at us that day in school was just a taste of the cultural clash that awaited us in the real world, where prospective employers and men on the street would often misinterpret our tight skirts and jingling bracelets as a "come-on."

Mixed cultural signals have perpetuated certain stereotypes—for   6 example, that of the Hispanic woman as the "hot tamale" or sexual firebrand. It is a one-dimensional view that the media have found easy to promote. In their special vocabulary, advertisers have designated "sizzling" and "smoldering" as the adjectives of choice for describing not only the foods but also the women of Latin America. From conversations in my house I recall hearing about the harassment that Puerto Rican women endured in factories where the "boss-men" talked to them as if sexual innuendo was all they understood, and worse, often gave them the choice of submitting to their advances or being fired.

It is custom, however, not chromosomes, that leads us to choose   7 scarlet over pale pink. As young girls, it was our mothers who influenced our decisions about clothes and colors—mothers who had grown up on a tropical island where the natural environment was a riot of primary colors, where showing your skin was one way to keep cool as well as to look sexy. Most important of all, on the island, women perhaps felt freer to dress and move more provocatively since, in most cases, they were protected by the traditions, mores, and laws of a Spanish/Catholic system of morality and machismo whose main rule was: *You may look at my sister, but if you touch her I will kill you.* The extended family and church structure could provide a young woman with a circle of safety in her small pueblo on the island; if a man "wronged" a girl, everyone would close in to save her family honor.

My mother has told me about dressing in her best party clothes   8 on Saturday nights and going to the town's plaza to promenade with her girlfriends in front of the boys they liked. The males were thus given an opportunity to admire the women and to express their admiration in the form of *piropos:* erotically charged street poems they composed on the spot. (I have myself been subjected to a few *piropos* while visiting the island, and they can be outrageous, although custom dictates that they must never cross into obscenity.) This ritual, as I understand it, also entails a show of studied indifference on the woman's part; if she is "decent," she must not acknowledge the man's impassioned words. So I do understand how things can be lost in translation. When a Puerto Rican girl dressed in her idea of what is attractive meets a man from the mainstream culture who has been trained to react to certain types of clothing as a sexual signal, a clash is likely to take place. I remember the boy who took me to my first formal dance leaning over to plant a sloppy, over-eager kiss painfully on my mouth; when I didn't respond with sufficient passion, he remarked resentfully: "I thought you Latin girls were supposed to mature early," as if I were expected to *ripen* like a fruit or vegetable, not just grow into womanhood like other girls.

It is surprising to my professional friends that even today some 9 people, including those who should know better, still put others "in their place." It happened to me most recently during a stay at a classy metropolitan hotel favored by young professional couples for weddings. Late one evening after the theater, as I walked toward my room with a colleague (a woman with whom I was coordinating an arts program), a middle-aged man in a tuxedo, with a young girl in satin and lace on his arm, stepped directly into our path. With his champagne glass extended toward me, he exclaimed "Evita!"[6]

Our way blocked, my companion and I listened as the man half- 10 recited, half-bellowed "Don't Cry for Me, Argentina." When he finished, the young girl said: "How about a round of applause for my daddy?" We complied, hoping this would bring the silly spectacle to a close. I was becoming aware that our little group was attracting the attention of the other guests. "Daddy" must have perceived this too, and he once more barred the way as we tried to walk past him. He began to shout-sing a ditty to the tune of "La Bamba"—except the lyrics were about a girl named Maria whose exploits rhymed with her name and gonorrhea. The girl kept saying "Oh, Daddy" and looking at me with pleading eyes. She wanted me to laugh along with the others. My companion and I stood silently waiting for the man to end his offensive song. When he finished, I looked not at him but at his daughter. I advised her calmly never to ask her father what he had done in the army. Then I walked between them and to my room. My friend complimented me on my cool handling of the situation, but I confessed that I had really wanted to push the jerk into the swimming pool. This same man—probably a corporate executive, well-educated, even worldly by most standards—would not have been likely to regale an Anglo woman with a dirty song in public. He might have checked his impulse by assuming that she could be somebody's wife or mother, or at least *somebody* who might take offense. But, to him, I was just an Evita or a Maria: merely a character in his cartoon-populated universe.

---

[6] A Broadway musical, later made into a movie, about Eva Duarte de Perón, the former first lady of Argentina.

Another facet of the myth of the Latin woman in the United States 11
is the menial, the domestic—Maria the housemaid or countergirl. It's
true that work as domestics, as waitresses, and in factories is all that's
available to women with little English and few skills. But the myth of
the Hispanic menial—the funny maid, mispronouncing words and
cooking up a spicy storm in a shiny California kitchen—has been perpetuated by the media in the same way that "Mammy" from *Gone with
the Wind* became America's idea of the black woman for generations.
Since I do not wear my diplomas around my neck for all to see, I have
on occasion been sent to that "kitchen" where some think I obviously
belong.

One incident has stayed with me, though I recognize it as a minor 12
offense. My first public poetry reading took place in Miami, at a
restaurant where a luncheon was being held before the event. I was
nervous and excited as I walked in with notebook in hand. An older
woman motioned me to her table, and thinking (foolish me) that she
wanted me to autograph a copy of my newly published slender vol-
ume of verse, I went over. She ordered a cup of coffee from me,
assuming that I was the waitress. (Easy enough to mistake my poems
for menus, I suppose.) I know it wasn't an intentional act of cruelty.
Yet of all the good things that happened later, I remember that scene
most clearly, because it reminded me of what I had to overcome
before anyone would take me seriously. In retrospect I understand
that my anger gave my reading fire. In fact, I have almost always
taken any doubt in my abilities as a challenge, the result most often
being the satisfaction of winning a convert, of seeing the cold, apprais-
ing eyes warm to my words, the body language change, the smile that
indicates I have opened some avenue for communication. So that day
as I read, I looked directly at that woman. Her lowered eyes told me
she was embarrassed at her faux pas, and when I willed her to look
up at me, she graciously allowed me to punish her with my full attention. We shook hands at the end of the reading and I never saw her
again. She has probably forgotten the entire incident, but maybe not.

Yet I am one of the lucky ones. There are thousands of Latinas 13
without the privilege of an education or the entrees into society that
I have. For them life is a constant struggle against the misconcep-
tions perpetuated by the myth of the Latina. My goal is to try to
replace the old stereotypes with a much more interesting set of realities. Every time I give a reading, I hope the stories I tell, the dreams
and fears I examine in my work, can achieve some universal truth
that will get my audience past the particulars of my skin color, my
accent, or my clothes.

COLLEGE PRESSURES

William Zinsser

Dear Carlos: I desperately need a dean's excuse for my chem midterm which will begin in about 1 hour. All I can say is that I totally blew it this week. I've fallen incredibly, inconceivably behind.

Carlos: Help! I'm anxious to hear from you. I'll be in my room and won't leave it until I hear from you. Tomorrow is the last day for . . .

Carlos: I left town because I started bugging out again. I stayed up all night to finish a take-home make-up exam & am typing it to hand in on the 10th. It was due on the 5th. P.S. I'm going to the dentist. Pain is pretty bad.

Carlos: Probably by Friday I'll be able to get back to my studies. Right now I'm going to take a long walk. This whole thing has taken a lot out of me.

Carlos: I'm really up the proverbial creek. The problem is I really *bombed* the history final. Since I need that course for my major I . . .

Carlos: Here follows a tale of woe. I went home this weekend, had to help my Mom, & caught a fever so didn't have much time to study. My professor . . .

Carlos: Aargh! Trouble. Nothing original but everything's piling up at once. To be brief, my job interview . . .

Hey Carlos, good news! I've got mononucleosis.

Who are these wretched supplicants, scribbling notes so laden 1 with anxiety, seeking such miracles of postponement and balm? They are men and women who belong to Branford College, one of the twelve residential colleges at Yale University, and the messages are just a few of the hundreds that they left for their dean, Carlos Hortas—often slipped under his door at 4 A.M.—last year.

But students like the ones who wrote those notes can also be 2
found on campuses from coast to coast—especially in New England
and at many other private colleges across the country that have high
academic standards and highly motivated students. Nobody could
doubt that the notes are real. In their urgency and their gallows
humor they are authentic voices of a generation that is panicky to
succeed.

My own connection with the message writers is that I am mas- 3
ter of Branford College. I live in its Gothic quadrangle and know the
students well. (We have 485 of them.) I am privy to their hopes and
fears—and also to their stereo music and their piercing cries in the
dead of night ("Does anybody *ca-a-are?*"). If they went to Carlos to
ask how to get through tomorrow, they come to me to ask how to get
through the rest of their lives.

Mainly I try to remind them that the road ahead is a long one and 4
that it will have more unexpected turns than they think. There will be
plenty of time to change jobs, change careers, change whole attitudes
and approaches. They don't want to hear such liberating news. They
want a map—right now—that they can follow unswervingly to career
security, financial security, Social Security and, presumably, a prepaid
grave.

What I wish for all students is some release from the clammy 5
grip of the future. I wish them a chance to savor each segment of their
education as an experience in itself and not as a grim preparation for
the next step. I wish them the right to experiment, to trip and fall, to
learn that defeat is as instructive as victory and is not the end of the
world.

My wish, of course, is naïve. One of the few rights that America 6
does not proclaim is the right to fail. Achievement is the national god,
venerated in our media—the million-dollar athlete, the wealthy executive—and glorified in our praise of possessions. In the presence of
such a potent state religion, the young are growing up old.

I see four kinds of pressure working on college students today: 7
economic pressure, parental pressure, peer pressure, and self-
induced pressure. It is easy to look around for villains—to blame the
colleges for charging too much money, the professors for assigning
too much work, the parents for pushing their children too far, the students for driving themselves too hard. But there are no villains; only
victims.

"In the late 1960s," one dean told me, "the typical question that I 8
got from students was 'Why is there so much suffering in the world?'
or 'How can I make a contribution?' Today it's 'Do you think it

would look better for getting into law school if I did a double major in history and political science, or just majored in one of them?'" Many other deans confirmed this pattern. One said: "They're trying to find an edge—the intangible something that will look better on paper if two students are about equal."

Note the emphasis on looking better. The transcript has become a   9 sacred document, the passport to security. How one appears on paper is more important than how one appears in person. *A* is for Admirable and *B* is for Borderline, even though, in Yale's official system of grading, *A* means "excellent" and *B* means "very good." Today, looking very good is no longer good enough, especially for students who hope to go on to law school or medical school. They know that entrance into the better schools will be an entrance into the better law firms and better medical practices where they will make a lot of money. They also know that the odds are harsh. Yale Law School, for instance, matriculates 170 students from an applicant pool of 3,700; Harvard enrolls 550 from a pool of 7,000.

It's all very well for those of us who write letters of recommen-   10 dation for our students to stress the qualities of humanity that will make them good lawyers or doctors. And it's nice to think that admission officers are really reading our letters and looking for the extra dimension of commitment or concern. Still, it would be hard for a student not to visualize these officers shuffling so many transcripts studded with *A*s that they regard a *B* as positively shameful.

The pressure is almost as heavy on students who just want to   11 graduate and get a job. Long gone are the days of the "gentleman's *C*," when students journeyed through college with a certain relaxation, sampling a wide variety of courses—music, art, philosophy, classics, anthropology, poetry, religion—that would send them out as liberally educated men and women. If I were an employer I would rather employ graduates who have this range and curiosity than those who narrowly pursued safe subjects and high grades. I know countless students whose inquiring minds exhilarate me. I like to hear the play of their ideas. I don't know if they are getting *A*s or *C*s, and I don't care. I also like them as people. The country needs them, and they will find satisfying jobs. I tell them to relax. They can't.

Nor can I blame them. They live in a brutal economy. Tuition,   12 room, and board at most private colleges now comes to at least $7,000, not counting books and fees. This might seem to suggest that the colleges are getting rich. But they are equally battered by inflation. Tuition covers only 60 percent of what it costs to educate a student, and ordinarily the remainder comes from what colleges receive in endowments, grants, and gifts. Now the remainder keeps being swallowed by the cruel costs—higher every year—of just opening the doors. Heating oil is up. Insurance is up. Postage is up. Health-premium costs are up. Everything is up. Deficits are up. We are witnessing in America the creation of a brotherhood of paupers— colleges, parents, and students, joined by the common bond of debt.

Today it is not unusual for a student, even if he works part time 13 at college and full time during the summer, to accrue $5,000 in loans after four years—loans that he must start to repay within one year after graduation. Exhorted at commencement to go forth into the world, he is already behind as he goes forth. How could he not feel under pressure throughout college to prepare for this day of reckoning? I have used "he," incidentally, only for brevity. Women at Yale are under no less pressure to justify their expensive education to themselves, their parents, and society. In fact, they are probably under more pressure. For although they leave college superbly equipped to bring fresh leadership to traditionally male jobs, society hasn't yet caught up with this fact.

Along with economic pressure goes parental pressure. 14 Inevitably, the two are deeply intertwined.

I see many students taking pre-medical courses with joyless 15 tenacity. They go off to their labs as if they were going to the dentist. It saddens me because I know them in other corners of their life as cheerful people.

"Do you want to go to medical school?" I ask them. 16

"I guess so," they say, without conviction, or "Not really." 17

"Then why are you going?" 18

"Well, my parents want me to be a doctor. They're paying all this 19 money and . . ."

Poor students, poor parents. They are caught in one of the oldest 20 webs of love and duty and guilt. The parents mean well; they are trying to steer their sons and daughters toward a secure future. But the sons and daughters want to major in history or classics or philosophy—subjects with no "practical" value. Where's the payoff on the humanities? It's not easy to persuade such loving parents that the humanities do indeed pay off. The intellectual faculties developed by studying subjects like history and classics—an ability to synthesize and relate, to weigh cause and effect, to see events in perspective— are just the faculties that make creative leaders in business or almost any general field. Still, many fathers would rather put their money on courses that point toward a specific profession—courses that are pre-law, pre-medical, pre-business, or, as I sometimes heard it put, "pre-rich."

But the pressure on students is severe. They are truly torn. One 21 part of them feels obligated to fulfill their parents' expectations; after all, their parents are older and presumably wiser. Another part tells them that the expectations that are right for their parents are not right for them.

I know a student who wants to be an artist. She is very obviously 22 an artist and will be a good one—she has already had several modest local exhibits. Meanwhile she is growing as a well-rounded person and taking humanistic subjects that will enrich the inner resources out of which her art will grow. But her father is strongly opposed. He thinks that an artist is a "dumb" thing to be. The student vacillates and tries to please everybody. She keeps up with her art somewhat furtively and takes some of the "dumb" courses her father wants her to take—at least they are dumb courses for her. She is a free spirit on a campus of tense students—no small achievement in itself—and she deserves to follow her muse.

Peer pressure and self-induced pressure are also intertwined, 23 and they begin almost at the beginning of freshman year.

"I had a freshman student I'll call Linda," one dean told me, "who 24 came in and said she was under terrible pressure because her roommate, Barbara, was much brighter and studied all the time. I couldn't tell her that Barbara had come in two hours earlier to say the same thing about Linda."

The story is almost funny—except that it's not. It's symptomatic 25 of all the pressures put together. When every student thinks every other student is working harder and doing better, the only solution is to study harder still. I see students going off to the library every night after dinner and coming back when it closes at midnight. I wish they would sometimes forget about their peers and go to a movie. I hear the clacking of typewriters in the hours before dawn. I see the tension in their eyes when exams are approaching and papers are due: *"Will I get everything done?"*

Probably they won't. They will get sick. They will get "blocked." 26 They will sleep. They will oversleep. They will bug out. *Hey Carlos, help!*

Part of the problem is that they do more than they are expected 27 to do. A professor will assign five-page papers. Several students will start writing ten-page papers to impress him. Then more students will write ten-page papers, and a few will raise the ante to fifteen. Pity the poor student who is still just doing the assignment.

"Once you have 20 or 30 percent of the student population deliberately overexerting," one dean points out, "it's bad for everybody. When a teacher gets more and more effort from his class, the student who is doing normal work can be perceived as not doing well. The tactic works, psychologically." 28

Why can't the professor just cut back and not accept longer papers? He can, and he probably will. But by then the term will be half over and the damage done. Grade fever is highly contagious and not easily reversed. Besides, the professor's main concern is with his course. He knows his students only in relation to the course and doesn't know that they are also overexerting in their other courses. Nor is it really his business. He didn't sign up for dealing with the student as a whole person and with all the emotional baggage the student brought along from home. That's what deans, masters, chaplains, and psychiatrists are for. 29

To some extent this is nothing new: a certain number of professors have always been self-contained islands of scholarship and shyness, more comfortable with books than with people. But the new pauperism has widened the gap still further, for professors who actually like to spend time with students don't have as much time to spend. They also are overexerting. If they are young, they are busy trying to publish in order not to perish, hanging by their finger nails onto a shrinking profession. If they are old and tenured, they are buried under the duties of administering departments—as departmental chairmen or members of committees—that have been thinned out by the budgetary axe. 30

Ultimately it will be the students' own business to break the circles in which they are trapped. They are too young to be prisoners of their parents' dreams and their classmates' fears. They must be jolted into believing in themselves as unique men and women who have the power to shape their own future. 31

"Violence is being done to the undergraduate experience," says Carlos Hortas. "College should be open-ended: at the end it should open many, many roads. Instead, students are choosing their goal in advance, and their choices narrow as they go along. It's almost as if they think that the country has been codified in the type of jobs that exist—that they've got to fit into certain slots. Therefore, fit into the best-paying slot. 32

"They ought to take chances. Not taking chances will lead to a life of colorless mediocrity. They'll be comfortable. But something in the spirit will be missing." 33

I have painted too drab a portrait of today's students, making 34
them seem a solemn lot. That is only half of their story; if they were
so dreary I wouldn't so thoroughly enjoy their company. The other
half is that they are easy to like. They are quick to laugh and to offer
friendship. They are not introverts. They are unusually kind and are
more considerate of one another than any student generation I have
known.

Nor are they so obsessed with their studies that they avoid sports 35
and extracurricular activities. On the contrary, they juggle their
crowded hours to play on a variety of teams, perform with musical
and dramatic groups, and write for campus publications. But this in
turn is one more cause of anxiety. There are too many choices.
Academically, they have 1,300 courses to select from; outside class
they have to decide how much spare time they can spare and how to
spend it.

This means that they engage in fewer extracurricular pursuits 36
than their predecessors did. If they want to row on the crew and play
in the symphony they will eliminate one; in the '60s they would have
done both. They also tend to choose activities that are self-limiting.
Drama, for instance, is flourishing in all twelve of Yale's residential
colleges as it never has before. Students hurl themselves into these
productions—as actors, directors, carpenters, and technicians—with a
dedication to create the best possible play, knowing that the day will
come when the run will end and they can get back to their studies.

They also can't afford to be the willing slave of organizations like 37
the *Yale Daily News.* Last spring at the one-hundredth anniversary
banquet of that paper—whose past chairmen include such once and
future kings as Potter Stewart,[1] Kingman Brewster,[2] and William F.
Buckley, Jr.[3]—much was made of the fact that the editorial staff used
to be small and totally committed and that "Newsies" routinely
worked fifty hours a week. In effect they belonged to a club; Newsies
is how they defined themselves at Yale. Today's student will write
one or two articles a week, when he can, and he defines himself as a
student. I've never heard the word Newsie except at the banquet.

---

[1] Potter Stewart was an associate justice of the U. S. Supreme Court.

[2] Kingman Brewster is a former president of Yale.

[3] William F. Buckley, Jr., is a columnist and founder of the conservative journal *The National Review.*

If I have described the modern undergraduate primarily as a dri- 38
ven creature who is largely ignoring the blithe spirit inside who
keeps trying to come out and play, it's because that's where the
crunch is, not only at Yale but throughout American education. It's
why I think we should all be worried about the values that are nur-
turing a generation so fearful of risk and so goal-obsessed at such an
early age.

I tell students that there is no one "right" way to get ahead—that 39
each of them is a different person, starting from a different point and
bound for a different destination. I tell them that change is a tonic
and that all the slots are not codified nor the frontiers closed. One of
my ways of telling them is to invite men and women who have
achieved success outside the academic world to come and talk infor-
mally with my students during the year. They are heads of companies or ad agencies, editors of magazines, politicians, public officials,
television magnates, labor leaders, business executives, Broadway
producers, artists, writers, economists, photographers, scientists, his-
torians—a mixed bag of achievers.

I ask them to say a few words about how they got started. The 40
students assume that they started in their present profession and
knew all along that it was what they wanted to do. Luckily for me,
most of them got into their field by a circuitous route, to their surprise, after many detours. The students are startled. They can hardly
conceive of a career that was not pre-planned. They can hardly imagine allowing the hand of God or chance to nudge them down some
unforeseen trail.

7

DEFINITION

WHY I WANT A WIFE

Judy Brady

I belong to that classification of people known as wives. I am A 1
Wife. And, not altogether incidentally, I am a mother.

Not too long ago a male friend of mine appeared on the scene 2
fresh from a recent divorce. He had one child, who is, of course, with
his ex-wife. He is looking for another wife. As I thought about him
while I was ironing one evening, it suddenly occurred to me that I,
too, would like to have a wife. Why do I want a wife?

I would like to go back to school so that I can become economi- 3
cally independent, support myself, and, if need be, support those
dependent upon me. I want a wife who will work and send me to
school. And while I am going to school I want a wife to take care of
my children. I want a wife to keep track of the children's doctor and
dentist appointments. And to keep track of mine, too. I want a wife
to make sure my children eat properly and are kept clean. I want a
wife who will wash the children's clothes and keep them mended. I
want a wife who is a good nurturant attendant to my children, who
arranges for their schooling, makes sure that they have an adequate
social life with their peers, takes them to the park, the zoo, etc. I want
a wife who takes care of the children when they are sick, a wife who
arranges to be around when the children need special care, because,
of course, I cannot miss classes at school. My wife must arrange to
lose time at work and not lose the job. It may mean a small cut in my
wife's income from time to time, but I guess I can tolerate that.
Needless to say, my wife will arrange and pay for the care of the children while my wife is working.

I want a wife who will take care of *my* physical needs. I want a 4
wife who will keep my house clean. A wife who will pick up after
me. I want a wife who will keep my clothes clean, ironed, mended,
replaced when need be, and who will see to it that my personal
things are kept in their proper place so that I can find what I need the
minute I need it. I want a wife who cooks the meals, a wife who is a
good cook. I want a wife who will plan the menus, do the necessary
grocery shopping, prepare the meals, serve them pleasantly, and then
do the cleaning up while I do my studying. I want a wife who will
care for me when I am sick and sympathize with my pain and loss of
time from school. I want a wife to go along when our family takes a
vacation so that someone can continue to care for me and my children when I need a rest and change of scene.

I want a wife who will not bother me with rambling complaints 5
about a wife's duties. But I want a wife who will listen to me when I
feel the need to explain a rather difficult point I have come across in
my course of studies. And I want a wife who will type my papers for
me when I have written them.

I want a wife who will take care of the details of my social life. 6
When my wife and I are invited out by friends, I want a wife who will
take care of the babysitting arrangements. When I meet people at
school that I like and want to entertain, I want a wife who will have the
house clean, will prepare a special meal, serve it to me and my friends,
and not interrupt when I talk about the things that interest me and my
friends. I want a wife who will have arranged that the children are fed
and ready for bed before my guests arrive so that the children do not
bother us. I want a wife who takes care of the needs of my guests so
that they feel comfortable, who makes sure that they have an ashtray,
that they are passed the hors d'oeuvres, that they are offered a second
helping of the food, that their wine glasses are replenished when necessary, that their coffee is served to them as they like it. And I want a
wife who knows that sometimes I need a night out by myself.

I want a wife who is sensitive to my sexual needs, a wife who 7
makes love passionately and eagerly when I feel like it, a wife who
makes sure that I am satisfied. And, of course, I want a wife who will
not demand sexual attention when I am not in the mood for it. I want
a wife who assumes the complete responsibility for birth control,
because I do not want more children. I want a wife who will remain
sexually faithful to me so that I do not have to clutter up my intellectual life with jealousies. And I want a wife who understands that *my*
sexual needs may entail more than strict adherence to monogamy. I
must, after all, be able to relate to people as fully as possible.

If, by chance, I find another person more suitable as a wife than   8
the wife I already have, I want the liberty to replace my present wife
with another one. Naturally, I will expect a fresh, new life; my wife
will take the children and be solely responsible for them so that I am
left free.

When I am through with school and have a job, I want my wife   9
to quit working and remain at home so that my wife can more fully
and completely take care of a wife's duties.

My God, who *wouldn't* want a wife?   10

MOTHER TONGUE

Amy Tan

I am not a scholar of English or literature. I cannot give you much [1] more than personal opinions on the English language and its variations in this country or others.

I am a writer. And by that definition, I am someone who has [2] always loved language. I am fascinated by language in daily life. I spend a great deal of my time thinking about the power of language—the way it can evoke an emotion, a visual image, a complex idea, or a simple truth. Language is the tool of my trade. And I use them all—all the Englishes I grew up with.

Recently, I was made keenly aware of the different Englishes I [3] do use. I was giving a talk to a large group of people, the same talk I had already given to half a dozen other groups. The nature of the talk was about my writing, my life, and my book, *The Joy Luck Club*. The talk was going along well enough, until I remembered one major difference that made the whole talk sound wrong. My mother was in the room. And it was perhaps the first time she had heard me give a lengthy speech, using the kind of English I have never used with her. I was saying things like, "The intersection of memory upon imagination" and "There is an aspect of my fiction that relates to thus-and-thus"—a speech filled with carefully wrought grammatical phrases, burdened, it suddenly seemed to me, with nominalized forms, past perfect tenses, conditional phrases, all the forms of standard English that I had learned in school and through books, the forms of English I did not use at home with my mother.

Just last week, I was walking down the street with my mother, [4] and I again found myself conscious of the English I was using, and the English I do use with her. We were talking about the price of new and used furniture and I heard myself saying this: "Not waste money that way." My husband was with us as well, and he didn't notice any switch in my English. And then I realized why. It's because over the twenty years we've been together I've often used that same kind of English with him, and sometimes he even uses it with me. It has become our language of intimacy, a different sort of English that relates to family talk, the language I grew up with.

So you'll have some idea of what this family talk I heard sounds [5] like, I'll quote what my mother said during a recent conversation which I videotaped and then transcribed. During this conversation, my mother was talking about a political gangster in Shanghai who had the same last name as her family's, Du, and how the gangster in his early years wanted to be adopted by her family, which was rich by comparison. Later, the gangster became more powerful, far richer than my mother's family, and one day showed up at my mother's wedding to pay his respects. Here's what she said in part:

"Du Yusong having business like fruit stand. Like off the street 6 kind. He is Du like Du Zong—but not Tsung-ming Island people. The local people call putong, the river east side, he belong to that side local people. The man want to ask Du Zong father take him in like become own family. Du Zong father wasn't look down on him, but didn't take seriously, until that man big like become a mafia. Now important person, very hard to inviting him. Chinese way, came only to show respect, don't stay for dinner. Respect for making big celebration, he shows up. Mean gives lots of respect. Chinese custom. Chinese social life that way. If too important won't have to stay too long. He come to my wedding. I didn't see, I heard it. I gone to boy's side, they have YMCA dinner. Chinese age I was nineteen."

You should know that my mother's expressive command of 7 English belies how much she actually understands. She reads the Forbes report, listens to *Wall Street Week*, converses daily with her stockbroker, reads all of Shirley MacLaine's[1] books with ease—all kinds of things I can't begin to understand. Yet some of my friends tell me they understand 50 percent of what my mother says. Some say they understand 80 to 90 percent. Some say they understand none of it, as if she were speaking pure Chinese. But to me, my mother's English is perfectly clear, perfectly natural. It's my mother tongue. Her language, as I hear it, is vivid, direct, full of observation and imagery. That was the language that helped shape the way I saw things, expressed things, made sense of the world.

Lately, I've been giving more thought to the kind of English my 8 mother speaks. Like others, I have described it to people as "broken" or "fractured" English. But I wince when I say that. It has always bothered me that I can think of no way to describe it other than "broken," as if it were damaged and needed to be fixed, as if it lacked a certain wholeness and soundness. I've heard other terms used, "limited English," for example. But they seem just as bad, as if everything is limited, including people's perceptions of the limited English speaker.

---

[1] Actress known for her autobiographical books, in which she traces her many past lives.

I know this for a fact, because when I was growing up, my   9
mother's "limited" English limited *my* perception of her. I was
ashamed of her English. I believed that her English reflected the quality of what she had to say. That is, because she expressed them imper-
fectly her thoughts were imperfect. And I had plenty of empirical
evidence to support me: the fact that people in department stores, at
banks, and at restaurants did not take her seriously, did not give her
good service, pretended not to understand her, or even acted as if
they did not hear her.

My mother has long realized the limitations of her English as well.   10
When I was fifteen, she used to have me call people on the phone to
pretend I was she. In this guise, I was forced to ask for information or
even to complain and yell at people who had been rude to her. One
time it was a call to her stockbroker in New York. She had cashed out
her small portfolio and it just so happened we were going to go to New
York the next week, our very first trip outside California. I had to get
on the phone and say in an adolescent voice that was not very convincing, "This is Mrs. Tan."

And my mother was standing in the back whispering loudly,   11
"Why he don't send me check, already two weeks late. So mad he lie
to me, losing me money."

And then I said in perfect English, "Yes, I'm getting rather   12
concerned. You had agreed to send the check two weeks ago, but it
hasn't arrived."

Then she began to talk more loudly. "What he want, I come to   13
New York tell him front of his boss, you cheating me?" And I was trying to calm her down, make her be quiet, while telling the stockbroker,
"I can't tolerate any more excuses. If I don't receive the check immediately, I am going to have to speak to your manager when I'm in New
York next week." And sure enough, the following week there we were
in front of this astonished stockbroker, and I was sitting there red-faced
and quiet, and my mother, the real Mrs. Tan, was shouting at his boss
in her impeccable broken English.

We used a similar routine just five days ago, for a situation that   14
was far less humorous. My mother had gone to the hospital for an
appointment, to find out about a benign brain tumor a CAT scan had
revealed a month ago. She said she had spoken very good English,
her best English, no mistakes. Still, she said, the hospital did not apol-
ogize when they said they had lost the CAT scan and she had come
for nothing. She said they did not seem to have any sympathy when
she told them she was anxious to know the exact diagnosis, since her
husband and son had both died of brain tumors. She said they would

not give her any more information until the next time and she would have to make another appointment for that. So she said she would not leave until the doctor called her daughter. She wouldn't budge. And when the doctor finally called her daughter, me, who spoke in perfect English—lo and behold—we had assurances the CAT scan would be found, promises that a conference call on Monday would be held, and apologies for any suffering my mother had gone through for a most regrettable mistake.

I think my mother's English almost had an effect on limiting my 15 possibilities in life as well. Sociologists and linguists probably will tell you that a person's developing language skills are more influenced by peers. But I do think that the language spoken in the family, especially in immigrant families which are more insular, plays a large role in shaping the language of the child. And I believe that it affected my results on achievement tests, IQ tests, and the SAT. While my English skills were never judged as poor, compared to math, English could not be considered my strong suit. In grade school I did moderately well, getting perhaps B's, sometimes B-pluses, in English and scoring perhaps in the sixtieth or seventieth percentile on achievement tests. But those scores were not good enough to override the opinion that my true abilities lay in math and science, because in those areas I achieved A's and scored in the ninetieth percentile or higher.

This was understandable. Math is precise; there is only one correct 16 answer. Whereas, for me at least, the answers on English tests were always a judgment call, a matter of opinion and personal experience. Those tests were constructed around items like fill-in-the-blank sentence completion, such as, "Even though Tom was   , Mary thought he was   ." And the correct answer always seemed to be the most bland combinations of thoughts, for example, "Even though Tom was shy, Mary thought he was charming," with the grammatical structure "even though" limiting the correct answer to some sort of semantic opposites, so you wouldn't get answers like, "Even though Tom was foolish, Mary thought he was ridiculous." Well, according to my mother, there were very few limitations as to what Tom could have been and what Mary might have thought of him. So I never did well on tests like that.

The same was true with word analogies, pairs of words in which 17 you were supposed to find some sort of logical, semantic relationship—for example, "*Sunset* is to *nightfall* as is to   ." And here you would be presented with a list of four possible pairs, one of which showed the same kind of relationship: *red* is to *stoplight, bus* is to *arrival, chills* is to *fever, yawn* is to *boring*. Well, I could never think that way. I knew what the tests were asking, but I could not block out of my mind the images already created by the first pair, *"sunset* is to *nightfall"*—and I would see a burst of colors against a darkening sky, the moon rising, the lowering of a curtain of stars. And all the other pairs of words— red, bus, stoplight, boring—just threw up a mass of confusing images, making it impossible for me to sort out something as logical as saying: "A sunset precedes nightfall" is the same as "a chill precedes a fever." The only way I would have gotten that answer right would have been to imagine an associative situation, for example, my being disobedient and staying out past sunset, catching a chill at night, which turns into feverish pneumonia as punishment, which indeed did happen to me.

I have been thinking about all this lately, about my mother's   18 English, about achievement tests. Because lately I've been asked, as a writer, why there are not more Asian Americans represented in American literature. Why are there few Asian Americans enrolled in creative writing programs? Why do so many Chinese students go into engineering? Well, these are broad sociological questions I can't begin to answer. But I have noticed in surveys—in fact, just last week—that Asian students, as a whole, always do significantly better on math achievement tests than in English. And this makes me think that there are other Asian-American students whose English spoken in the home might also be described as "broken" or "limited." And perhaps they also have teachers who are steering them away from writing and into math and science, which is what happened to me.

Fortunately, I happen to be rebellious in nature and enjoy the chal-   19 lenge of disproving assumptions made about me. I became an English major my first year in college, after being enrolled as pre-med. I started writing nonfiction as a freelancer the week after I was told by my former boss that writing was my worst skill and I should hone my talents toward account management.

But it wasn't until 1985 that I finally began to write fiction. And   20 at first I wrote using what I thought to be wittily crafted sentences, sentences that would finally prove I had mastery over the English language. Here's an example from the first draft of a story that later made its way into *The Joy Luck Club,* but without this line: "That was my mental quandary in its nascent state." A terrible line, which I can barely pronounce.

Fortunately, for reasons I won't get into today, I later decided   21 I should envision a reader for the stories I would write. And the reader I decided upon was my mother, because these were stories about mothers. So with this reader in mind—and in fact she did read my early drafts—I began to write stories using all the Englishes I grew up with: the English I spoke to my mother, which for lack of a better term might be described as "simple"; the English she used with me, which for lack of a better term might be described as "broken"; my translation of her Chinese, which could certainly be described as "watered down"; and what I imagined to be her translation of her Chinese if she could speak in perfect English, her internal language, and for that I sought to preserve the essence, but neither an English nor a Chinese structure. I wanted to capture what language ability tests can never reveal: her intent, her passion, her imagery, the rhythms of her speech and the nature of her thoughts.

Apart from what any critic had to say about my writing, I knew 22 I had succeeded where it counted when my mother finished reading my book and gave me her verdict: "So easy to read."

THE BARRIO

Robert Ramirez

The train, its metal wheels squealing as they spin along the sil- 1
very tracks, rolls slower now. Through the gaps between the cars
blinks a streetlamp, and this pulsing light on a barrio street corner
beats slower, like a weary heartbeat, until the train shudders to a halt,
the light goes out, and the barrio is deep asleep.

Throughout Aztlán (the Nahuatl term meaning "land to the 2
north"), trains grumble along the edges of a sleeping people. From
Lower California, through the blistering Southwest, down the Rio
Grande to the muddy Gulf, the darkness and mystery of dreams
engulf communities fenced off by railroads, canals, and expressways.
Paradoxical communities, isolated from the rest of the town by concrete columned monuments of progress, and yet stranded in the past.
They are surrounded by change. It eludes their reach, in their own
backyards, and the people, unable and unwilling to see the future, or
even touch the present, perpetuate the past.

Leaning from the expressway or jolting across the tracks, one 3
enters a different physical world permeated by a different attitude.
The physical dimensions are impressive. It is a large section of town
which extends for fifteen blocks north and south along the tracks,
and then advances eastward, thinning into nothingness beyond the
city limits. Within the invisible (yet sensible) walls of the barrio are
many, many people living in too few houses. The homes, however,
are much more numerous than on the outside.

Members of the barrio describe the entire area as their home. It is 4
a home, but it is more than this. The barrio is a refuge from the harsh-
ness and the coldness of the Anglo world. It is a forced refuge. The
leprous people are isolated from the rest of the community and con-
tained in their section of town. The stoical pariahs of the barrio accept
their fate, and from the angry seeds of rejection grow the flowers of
closeness between outcasts, not the thorns of bitterness and the mad
desire to flee. There is no want to escape, for the feeling of the barrio
is known only to its inhabitants, and the material needs of life can
also be found here.

The *tortillería* fires up its machinery three times a day, producing 5
steaming, round, flat slices of barrio bread. In the winter, the warmth

of the tortilla factory is a wool sarape in the chilly morning hours, but in the summer, it unbearably toasts every noontime customer.

The *panadería* sends its sweet messenger aroma down the dimly ₆ lit street, announcing the arrival of fresh, hot, sugary *pan dulce*.

The small corner grocery serves the meal-to-meal needs of cus- ₇ tomers, and the owner, a part of the neighborhood, willingly gives credit to people unable to pay cash for foodstuffs.

The barbershop is a living room with hydraulic chairs, radio, and ₈ television, where old friends meet and speak of life as their salted hair falls aimlessly about them.

The pool hall is a junior level country club where *'chucos*, ₉ strangers in their own land, get together to shoot pool and rap, while veterans, unaware of the cracking, popping balls on the green felt, complacently play dominoes beneath rudely hung *Playboy* foldouts.

The *cantina* is the night spot of the barrio. It is the country club ₁₀ and the den where the rites of puberty are enacted. Here the young become men. It is in the taverns that a young dude shows his *machismo* through the quantity of beer he can hold, the stories of *rucas* he has had, and his willingness and ability to defend his image against hardened and scarred old lions.

No, there is no frantic wish to flee. It would be absurd to leave ₁₁ the familiar and nervously step into the strange and cold Anglo community when the needs of the Chicano can be met in the barrio.

The barrio is closeness. From the family living unit, familial rela- ₁₂ tionships stretch out to immediate neighbors, down the block, around the corner, and to all parts of the barrio. The feeling of family, a rare and treasurable sentiment, pervades and accounts for the inability of the people to leave. The barrio is this attitude manifested on the countenances of the people, on the faces of their homes, and in the gaiety of their gardens.

The color-splashed homes arrest your eyes, arouse your curios- ₁₃ ity, and make you wonder what life scenes are being played out in them. The flimsy, brightly colored, wood-frame houses ignore no neon-brilliant color. Houses trimmed in orange, chartreuse, lime green, yellow, and mixtures of these and other hues beckon the beholder to reflect on the peculiarity of each home. Passing through this land is refreshing like Brubeck, not narcoticizing like revolting rows of similar houses, which neither offend nor please.

In the evenings, the porches and front yards are occupied with ₁₄ men calmly talking over the noise of children playing baseball in the unpaved extension of the living room, while the women cook supper or gossip with female neighbors as they water the *jardines*. The gardens mutely echo the expressive verses of the colorful houses. The denseness of multicolored plants and trees gives the house the appearance of an oasis or a tropical isand hideaway, sheltered from the rest of the world.

Fences are common in the barrio, but they are fences and not the 15 walls of the Anglo community. On the western side of town, the high wooden fences between houses are thick, impenetrable walls, built to keep the neighbors at bay. In the barrio, the fences may be rusty, wire contraptions or thick green shrubs. In either case you can see through them and feel no sense of intrusion when you cross them.

Many lower-income families of the barrio manage to maintain a 16 comfortable standard of living through the communal action of family members who contribute their wages to the head of the family. Economic need creates interdependence and closeness. Small bare-footed boys sell papers on cool, dark Sunday mornings, deny themselves pleasantries, and give their earnings to *mamá*. The older the child, the greater the responsibility to help the head of the household provide for the rest of the family.

There are those, too, who for a number of reasons have not 17 achieved a relative sense of financial security. Perhaps it results from too many children too soon, but it is the homes of these people and their situation that numbs rather than charms. Their houses, aged and bent, oozing children, are fissures in the horn of plenty. Their wooden homes may have brick-pattern asbestos tile on the outer walls, but the tile is not convincing.

Unable to pay city taxes or incapable of influencing the city to 18 live up to its duty to serve all the citizens, the poorer barrio families remain trapped in the nineteenth century and survive as best they can. The backyards have well-worn paths to the outhouses, which sit near the alley. Running water is considered a luxury in some parts of the barrio. Decent drainage is usually unknown, and when it rains, the water stands for days, an incubator of health hazards and an avoidable nuisance. Streets, costly to pave, remain rough, rocky trails. Tires do not last long, and the constant rattling and shaking grind away a car's life and spread dust through screen windows.

The houses and their *jardines*, the jollity of the people in an 19 adverse world, the brightly feathered alarm clock pecking away at supper and cautiously eyeing the children playing nearby, produce a mystifying sensation at finding the noble savage alive in the twentieth century. It is easy to look at the positive qualities of life in the barrio and look at them with a distantly envious feeling. One wishes to experience the feelings of the barrio and not the hardships.

Remembering the illness, the hunger, the feeling of time running out on you, the walls, both real and imagined, reflecting on living in the past, one finds his envy becoming more elusive, until it has vanished altogether.

Back now beyond the tracks, the train creaks and groans, the cars jostle each other down the track, and as the light begins its pulsing, the barrio, with all its meanings, greets a new dawn with yawns and restless stretchings. 20

8

EXEMPLIFICATION

JUST WALK ON BY: A BLACK MAN PONDERS HIS POWER TO ALTER PUBLIC SPACE

Brent Staples

My first victim was a woman—white, well dressed, probably in 1
her early twenties. I came upon her late one evening on a deserted
street in Hyde Park, a relatively affluent neighborhood in an otherwise mean, impoverished section of Chicago. As I swung onto the
avenue behind her, there seemed to be a discreet, uninflammatory
distance between us. Not so. She cast back a worried glance. To her,
the youngish black man—a broad six feet two inches with a beard
and billowing hair, both hands shoved into the pockets of a bulky
military jacket—seemed menacingly close. After a few more quick
glimpses, she picked up her pace and was soon running in earnest.
Within seconds she disappeared into a cross street.

That was more than a decade ago. I was 22 years old, a graduate 2
student newly arrived at the University of Chicago. It was in the echo
of that terrified woman's footfalls that I first began to know the
unwieldy inheritance I'd come into—the ability to alter public space
in ugly ways. It was clear that she thought herself the quarry of a
mugger, rapist, or worse. Suffering a bout of insomnia, however, I
was stalking sleep, not defenseless wayfarers. As a softy who is
scarcely able to take a knife to a raw chicken—let alone hold it to a
person's throat—I was surprised, embarrassed, and dismayed all at
once. Her flight made me feel like an accomplice in tyranny. It also
made it clear that I was indistinguishable from the muggers who
occasionally seeped into the area from the surrounding ghetto. That
first encounter, and those that followed, signified that a vast, unnerving gulf lay between nighttime pedestrians—particularly women—

and me. And I soon gathered that being perceived as dangerous is a hazard in itself. I only needed to turn a corner into a dicey situation or crowd some frightened, armed person in a foyer somewhere, or make an errant move after being pulled over by a policeman. Where fear and weapons meet—and they often do in urban America—there is always the possibility of death.

In that first year, my first away from my hometown, I was to become thoroughly familiar with the language of fear. At dark, shadowy intersections in Chicago, I could cross in front of a car stopped at a traffic light and elicit the *thunk, thunk, thunk, thunk* of the driver— black, white, male or female—hammering down the door locks. On less traveled streets after dark, I grew accustomed to but never comfortable with people who crossed to the other side of the street rather than pass me. Then there were the standard unpleasantries with police, doormen, bouncers, cab drivers, and others whose business it is to screen out troublesome individuals *before* there is any nastiness.

I moved to New York nearly two years ago and I have remained an avid night walker. In central Manhattan, the near-constant crowd cover minimizes tense one-on-one street encounters. Elsewhere—visiting friends in SoHo, where sidewalks are narrow and tightly spaced buildings shut out the sky—things can get very taut indeed.

Black men have a firm place in New York mugging literature. Norman Podhoretz in his famed (or infamous) 1963 essay, "My Negro Problem—and Ours," recalls growing up in terror of black males; they "were tougher than we were, more ruthless," he writes— and as an adult on the Upper West Side of Manhattan, he continues, he cannot constrain his nervousness when he meets black men on certain streets. Similarly, a decade later, the essayist and novelist Edward Hoagland extols a New York where once "Negro bitterness bore down mainly on other Negroes." Where some see mere panhandlers, Hoagland sees "a mugger who is clearly screwing up his nerve to do more than just *ask* for money." But Hoagland has "the New Yorker's quick-hunch posture for broken-field maneuvering," and the bad guy swerves away.

I often witness that "hunch posture," from women after dark on the warrenlike streets of Brooklyn where I live. They seem to set their faces on neutral and, with their purse straps strung across their chests bandolier style, they forge ahead as though bracing themselves against being tackled. I understand, of course, that the danger they perceive is not a hallucination. Women are particularly vulnerable to street violence, and young black males are drastically overrepresented among the perpetrators of that violence. Yet these truths are no solace against the kind of alienation that comes of being ever the suspect, against being set apart, a fearsome entity with whom pedestrians avoid making eye contact.

It is not altogether clear to me how I reached the ripe old age of 22 7 without being conscious of the lethality nighttime pedestrians attributed to me. Perhaps it was because in Chester, Pennsylvania, the small, angry industrial town where I came of age in the 1960s, I was scarcely noticeable against a backdrop of gang warfare, street knifings, and murders. I grew up one of the good boys, had perhaps a half-dozen fist fights. In retrospect, my shyness of combat has clear sources.

Many things go into the making of a young thug. One of those 8 things is the consummation of the male romance with the power to intimidate. An infant discovers that random flailings send the baby bottle flying out of the crib and crashing to the floor. Delighted, the joyful babe repeats those motions again and again, seeking to duplicate the feat. Just so, I recall the points at which some of my boyhood friends were finally seduced by the perception of themselves as tough guys. When a mark cowered and surrendered his money without resistance, myth and reality merged—and paid off. It is, after all, only manly to embrace the power to frighten and intimidate. We, as men, are not supposed to give an inch of our lane on the highway; we are to seize the fighter's edge in work and in play and even in love; we are to be valiant in the face of hostile forces.

Unfortunately, poor and powerless young men seem to take all 9 this nonsense literally. As a boy, I saw countless tough guys locked away; I have since buried several, too. They were babies, really—a teenage cousin, a brother of 22, a childhood friend in his mid-twenties—all gone down in episodes of bravado played out in the streets. I came to doubt the virtues of intimidation early on. I chose, perhaps even unconsciously, to remain a shadow—timid, but a survivor.

The fearsomeness mistakenly attributed to me in public places 10 often has a perilous flavor. The most frightening of these confusions occurred in the late 1970s and early 1980s when I worked as a journalist in Chicago. One day, rushing into the office of a magazine I was writing for with a deadline story in hand, I was mistaken for a burglar. The office manager called security and, with an ad hoc posse, pursued me through the labyrinthine halls, nearly to my editor's door. I had no way of proving who I was. I could only move briskly toward the company of someone who knew me.

Another time I was on assignment for a local paper and killing 11 time before an interview. I entered a jewelry store on the city's affluent Near North Side. The proprietor excused herself and returned with an enormous red Doberman pinscher straining at the end of a leash. She stood, the dog extended toward me, silent to my questions, her eyes bulging nearly out of her head. I took a cursory look around, nodded, and bade her good night. Relatively speaking, however, I never fared as badly as another black male journalist. He went to nearby Waukegan, Illinois, a couple of summers ago to work on a story about a murderer who was born there. Mistaking the reporter for the killer, police hauled him from his car at gunpoint and but for his press credentials would probably have tried to book him. Such episodes are not uncommon. Black men trade tales like this all the time.

In "My Negro Problem—and Ours," Podhoretz writes that the 12
hatred he feels for blacks makes itself known to him through a variety of avenues—one being his discomfort with that "special brand of paranoid touchiness" to which he says blacks are prone. No doubt he is speaking here of black men. In time, I learned to smother the rage I felt at so often being taken for a criminal. Not to do so would surely have led to madness—via that special "paranoid touchiness" that so annoyed Podhoretz at the time he wrote the essay.

I began to take precautions to make myself less threatening. I 13
move about with care, particularly late in the evening. I give a wide berth to nervous people on subway platforms during the wee hours, particularly when I have exchanged business clothes for jeans. If I happen to be entering a building behind some people who appear skittish, I may walk by, letting them clear the lobby before I return, so as not to seem to be following them. I have been calm and extremely congenial on those rare occasions when I've been pulled over by the police.

And on late-evening constitutionals along streets less traveled 14
by, I employ what has proved to be an excellent tension-reducing measure: I whistle melodies from Beethoven and Vivaldi and the more popular classical composers. Even steely New Yorkers hunching toward nighttime destinations seem to relax, and occasionally they even join in the tune. Virtually everybody seems to sense that a mugger wouldn't be warbling bright, sunny selections from Vivaldi's *Four Seasons*. It is my equivalent of the cowbell that hikers wear when they know they are in bear country.

ON THE INTERSTATE:
A CITY OF THE MIND

Sue Hubbell

In the early morning there is a city of the mind that stretches 1
from coast to coast, from border to border. Its cross streets are the
interstate highways, and food, comfort, companionship are served
up in its buildings, the truck stops near the exits. Its citizens are all-
night drivers, the truckers, and the waitresses at the stops.

In the daylight the city fades and blurs when the transients 2
appear, tourists who merely want a meal and a tank of gas. They file
into the carpeted dining rooms away from the professional drivers'
side, sit at the Formica tables set off by imitation cloth flowers in bud
vases. They eat and are gone, do not return. They are not a part of the
city and obscure it.

It is 5 A.M. in a truck stop in West Virginia. Drivers in twos, threes, 3
and fours are eating breakfast and talking routes and schedules.

"Truckers!" growls a manager. "They say they are in a hurry. 4
They complain if the service isn't fast. We fix it so they can have their
fuel pumped while they are eating and put in telephones on every
table so they can check with their dispatchers at the same time. They
could be out of here in half an hour. But what do they do? They sit
and talk for two hours."

The truckers are lining up for seconds at the breakfast buffet (all 5
you can eat for $3.99—biscuits with chipped-beef gravy, fruit cup,
French toast with syrup, bacon, pancakes, sausage, scrambled eggs,
doughnuts, Danish, cereal in little boxes).

The travel store at the truck stop has a machine to measure heart- 6
beat in exchange for a quarter. There are racks of jackets, belts, truck
supplies, tape cassettes. On the wall are paintings for sale, simulated
wood with likenesses of John Wayne or a stag. The rack by the cash
register is stuffed with Twinkies and chocolate Suzy Qs.

It is 5 A.M. in New Mexico. Above the horseshoe-shaped counter 7
on panels where a menu is usually displayed, an overhead slide
show is in progress. The pictures change slowly, allowing the viewer
to take in all the details. A low shot of a Peterbilt, its chrome fittings
sparkling in the sunshine, is followed by one of a bosomy young
woman, the same who must pose for those calendars found in
autoparts stores. She almost has on clothes, and she is offering to
check a trucker's oil. The next slide is a side view of a whole tractor-

trailer rig, its 18 wheels gleaming and spoked. It is followed by one of a blond bulging out of a hint of cop clothes writing a naughty trucker a ticket.

The waitress looks too tired and too jaded to be offended. The jaws of the truckers move mechanically as they fork up their eggs-over-easy. They stare at the slides, glassy eyed, as intent on chrome as on flesh. 8

It is 4 A.M. in Oklahoma. A recycled Stuckey's with blue tile roof calls itself simply Truck Stop. The sign also boasts showers, scales, truck wash and a special on service for $88.50. At a table inside, four truckers have ordered a short stack and three eggs a piece, along with bacon, sausage, and coffee (Trucker's Superbreakfast—$3.79). 9

They have just started drinking their coffee, and the driver with the Roadway cap calls over the waitress, telling her there is salt in the sugar he put in his coffee. She is pale, thin, young, has dark circles under her eyes. The truckers have been teasing her, and she doesn't trust them. She dabs a bit of sugar from the canister on a finger and tastes it. Salt. She samples sugar from the other canisters. They have salt too, and she gathers them up to replace them. Someone is hazing her, breaking her into her new job. Her eyes shine with tears. 10

She brings the food and comes back when the truckers are nearly done. She carries a water jug and coffeepot on her tray. The men are ragging her again, and her hands tremble. The tray falls with a crash. The jug breaks. Glass, water, and coffee spread across the floor. She sits down in the booth, tears rolling down her cheeks. 11

"I'm so tired. My old man . . . he left me," she says, the tears coming faster now. "The judge says he's going to take my kid away if I can't take care of him, so I stay up all day and just sleep when he takes a nap and the boss yells at me and . . . and . . . the truckers all talk dirty . . . I'm so tired." 12

She puts her head down on her arms and sobs luxuriantly. The truckers are gone, and I touch her arm and tell her to look at what they have left. There is a $20 bill beside each plate. She looks up, nods, wipes her eyes on her apron, pockets the tips, and goes to get a broom and a mop. 13

It is 3:30 A.M. in Illinois at a glossy truck stop that offers all mechanical services, motel rooms, showers, Laundromat, game room, TV lounge, truckers' bulletin board, and a stack of newspapers published by the Association of Christian Truckers. Piped-in music fills the air. 14

The waitress in the professional drivers' section is a big moth-erly-looking woman with red hair piled in careful curls on top of her 15 head. She correctly sizes up the proper meal for the new customer at the counter. "Don't know what you want, honey? Try the chicken-noodle soup with a hot roll. It will stick to you like you've got something, and you don't have to worry about grease."

She has been waitressing 40 years, 20 of them in this truck stop. 16 As she talks she polishes the stainless steel, fills mustard jars, adds the menu inserts for today's special (hot turkey sandwich, mashed potatoes and gravy, pot of coffee—$2.50).

"The big boss, well, he's a love, but some of the others aren't so 17 hot. But it's a job. Gotta work somewhere. I need a day off though. Been working six, seven days straight lately. Got shopping to do. My lawn needs mowing."

Two truckers are sitting at a booth. Their faces are lined and 18 leathery. One cap says HARLEY-DAVIDSON, the other COORS.

Harley-Davidson calls out, "If you wasn't so mean, Flossie, 19 you'd have a good man to take care of you and you wouldn't have to mow the damn lawn."

She puts down the mustard jar, walks over to Harley-Davidson 20 and Coors, stands in front of them, hands on wide hips. "Now you listen here, Charlie, I'm a good enough woman for any man, but all you guys want are chippies."

Coors turns bright red. She glares at him. "You saw my ex in here 21 last Saturday night with a chippie on his arm. He comes in here all the time with two, three chippies just to prove to me what a high old time he's having. If that's a good time, I'd rather baby-sit my grand-kids."

Chippies are not a topic of conversation that Charlie and Coors 22 wish to pursue. Coors breaks a doughnut in two, and Charlie uses his fork to make a spillway for the gravy on the double order of mashed potatoes that accompanies his scrambled eggs.

Flossie comes back to the counter and turns to the new customer 23 in mirror shades at this dark hour, a young trucker with cowboy boots and hat. "John boy. Where you been? Haven't seen you in weeks. Looks like you need a nice omelet. Cook just made some of those biscuits you like too."

I leave a tip for Flossie and pay my bill. In the men's room, where 24 I am shunted because the ladies' is closed for cleaning, someone has scrawled poignant words: NO TIME TO EAT NOW.

A WEIGHT THAT WOMEN CARRY

Sallie Tisdale

I don't know how much I weigh these days, though I can make 1
a good guess. For years I'd known that number, sometimes within a
quarter pound, known how it changed from day to day and hour to
hour. I want to weigh myself now; I lean toward the scale in the next
room, imagine standing there, lining up the balance. But I don't do it.
Going this long, starting to break the scale's spell—it's like waking
up suddenly sober.

By the time I was sixteen years old I had reached my adult height 2
of five feet six inches and weighed 164 pounds. I weighed 164
pounds before and after a healthy pregnancy. I assume I weigh about
the same now; nothing significant seems to have happened to my
body, this same old body I've had all these years. I usually wear a size
14, a common clothing size for American women. On bad days I
think my body looks lumpy and misshapen. On my good days,
which are more frequent lately, I think I look plush and strong; I think
I look like a lot of women whose bodies and lives I admire.

I'm not sure when the word "fat" first sounded pejorative to me, 3
or when I first applied it to myself. My grandmother was a petite
woman, the only one in my family. She stole food from other people's
plates, and hid the debris of her own meals so that no one would
know how much she ate. My mother was a size 14, like me, all her
adult life; we shared clothes. She fretted endlessly over food scales,
calorie counters, and diet books. She didn't want to quit smoking
because she was afraid she would gain weight, and she worried about
her weight until she died of cancer five years ago. Dieting was always
in my mother's way, always there in the conversations above my
head, the dialogue of stocky women. But I was strong and healthy
and didn't pay too much attention to my weight until I was grown.

It probably wouldn't have been possible for me to escape forever. 4
It doesn't matter that whole human epochs have celebrated big men
and women, because the brief period in which I live does not; since I
was born, even the voluptuous calendar girl has gone. Today's models, the women whose pictures I see constantly, unavoidably, grow
more minimal by the day. When I berate myself for not looking like—
whomever I think I should look like that day, I don't really care that
no one looks like that. I don't care that Michelle Pfeiffer doesn't look
like the photographs I see of Michelle Pfeiffer. I want to look—think

I should look—like the photographs. I want her little miracles: the makeup artists, photographers, and computer imagers who can add a mole, remove a scar, lift the breasts, widen the eyes, narrow the hips, flatten the curves. The final product is what I see, have seen my whole adult life. And I've seen this: even when big people become celebrities, their weight is constantly remarked upon and scrutinized; their successes seem always to be *in spite of* their weight. I thought my successes must be, too.

I feel myself expand and diminish from day to day, sometimes 5 from hour to hour. If I tell someone my weight, I change in their eyes: I become bigger or smaller, better or worse, depending on what that number, my weight, means to them. I know many men and women, young and old, gay and straight, who look fine, whom I love to see and whose faces and forms I cherish, who despise themselves for their weight. For their ordinary, human bodies. They and I are simply bigger than we think we should be. We always talk about weight in terms of gains and losses, and don't wonder at the strangeness of the words. In trying always to lose weight, we've lost hope of simply being seen for ourselves.

My weight has never actually affected anything—it's never 6 seemed to mean anything one way or the other to how I lived. Yet for the last ten years I've felt quite bad about it. After a time, the number on the scale became my totem, more important than my experience— it was layered, metaphorical, *metaphysical*, and it had bewitching power. I thought if I could change that number I could change my life.

In my mid-twenties I started secretly taking diet pills. They made 7 me feel strange, half-crazed, vaguely nauseated. I lost about twenty-five pounds, dropped two sizes, and bought new clothes. I developed rituals and taboos around food, ate very little, and continued to lose weight. For a long time afterward I thought it only coincidental that with every passing week I also grew more depressed and irritable.

I could recite the details, but they're remarkable only for being so 8 common. I lost more weight until I was rather thin, and then I gained it all back. It came back slowly, pound by pound, in spite of erratic and melancholy and sometimes frantic dieting, dieting I clung to even though being thin had changed nothing, had meant nothing to my life except that I was thin. Looking back, I remember blinding moments of shame and lightning-bright moments of clearheaded-ness, which inevitably gave way to rage at the time I'd wasted—rage that eventually would become, once again, self-disgust and the urge to lose weight. So it went, until I weighed exactly what I'd weighed when I began.

I used to be attracted to the sharp angles of the chronic dieter—the 9 caffeine-wild, chain-smoking, skinny women I see sometimes. I considered them a pinnacle not of beauty but of will. Even after I gained back my weight, I wanted to be like that, controlled and persevering, live that underfed life so unlike my own rather sensual and disorderly existence. I felt I should always be dieting, for the dieting of it; dieting had become a rule, a given, a constant. Every ordinary value is distorted in this lens. I felt guilty for not being completely absorbed in my diet, for getting distracted, for not caring enough all the time. The fat person's character flaw is a lack of narcissism. She's let herself go.

So I would begin again—and at first it would all seem so . . . . 10 easy. Simple arithmetic. After all, 3,500 calories equal one pound of fat—so the books and articles by the thousands say. I would calculate how long it would take to achieve the magic number on the scale, to succeed, to win. All past failures were suppressed. If 3,500 calories equal one pound, all I needed to do was cut 3,500 calories out of my intake every week. The first few days of a new diet would be colored with a sense of control—organization and planning, power over the self. Then the basic futile misery took over.

I would weigh myself with foreboding, and my weight would 11 determine how went the rest of my day, my week, my life. When 3,500 calories didn't equal one pound lost after all, I figured it was my body that was flawed, not the theory. One friend, who had tried for years to lose weight following prescribed diets, made what she called "an amazing discovery." The real secret to a diet, she said, was that you had to be willing to be hungry *all the time.* You had to eat even less than the diet allowed.

I believed that being thin would make me happy. Such a perni- 12 cious, enduring belief. I lost weight and wasn't happy and saw that elusive happiness disappear in a vanishing point, requiring more—more self-disgust, more of the misery of dieting. Knowing all that I know now about the biology and anthropology of weight, knowing that people naturally come in many shapes and sizes, knowing that diets are bad for me and won't make me thin—sometimes none of this matters. I look in the mirror and think: Who am I kidding? *I've got to do something about myself.* Only then will this vague discontent disappear. Then I'll be loved [. . .].

Fat is perceived as an *act* rather than a thing. It is antisocial, and 13 curable through the application of social controls. Even the feminist revisions of dieting, so powerful in themselves, pick up the theme: the hungry, empty heart; the woman seeking release from sexual assault, or the man from the loss of the mother, through food and fat. Fat is now a symbol not of the personality but of the soul—the cluttered, neurotic, immature soul.

Fat people eat for "mere gratification," I read, as though no one else does. Their weight is *intentioned*, they simply eat "too much," their flesh is lazy flesh. Whenever I went on a diet, eating became cheating. One pretzel was cheating. Two apples instead of one was cheating—a large potato instead of a small, carrots instead of broccoli. It didn't matter which diet I was on; diets have failure built in, failure is in the definition. Every substitution—even carrots for broccoli—was a triumph of desire over will. When I dieted, I didn't feel pious just for sticking to the rules. I felt condemned for the act of eating itself, as though my hunger were never normal. My penance was to not eat at all.

My attitude toward food became quite corrupt. I came, in fact, to subconsciously believe food itself was corrupt. Diet books often distinguish between "real" and "unreal" hunger, so that *correct* eating is hollowed out, unemotional. A friend of mine who thinks of herself as a compulsive eater says she feels bad only when she eats for pleasure. "Why?" I ask, and she says, "Because I'm eating food I don't need." A few years ago I might have admired that. Now I try to imagine a world where we eat only food we need, and it seems inhuman. I imagine a world devoid of holidays and wedding feasts, wakes and reunions, a unique shared joy. "What's wrong with eating a cookie because you like cookies?" I ask her, and she hasn't got an answer. These aren't rational beliefs, any more than the unnecessary pleasure of ice cream is rational. Dieting presumes pleasure to be an insignificant, or at least malleable, human motive.

I felt no joy in being thin—it was just work, something I had to do. But when I began to gain back the weight, I felt despair. I started reading about the "recidivism" of dieting. I wondered if I had myself to blame not only for needing to diet in the first place but for dieting itself, the weight inevitably regained. I joined organized weight-loss programs, spent a lot of money, listened to lectures I didn't believe on quack nutrition, ate awful, processed diet foods. I sat in groups and applauded people who'd lost a half pound, feeling smug because I'd lost a pound and a half. I felt ill much of the time, found exercise increasingly difficult, cried often. And I thought that if I could only lose a little weight, everything would be all right [. . .].

Recently I was talking with a friend who is naturally slender about a mutual acquaintance who is quite large. To my surprise my friend reproached this woman because she had seen her eating a cookie at lunchtime. "How is she going to lose weight that way?" my friend wondered. When you are as fat as our acquaintance is, you are primarily, fundamentally, seen as fat. It is your essential characteristic. There are so many presumptions in my friend's casual, cruel remark. She assumes that this woman should diet all the time—and that she *can*. She pronounces whole categories of food to be denied her. She sees her unwillingness to behave in this externally prescribed way, even for a moment, as an act of rebellion. In his story "A Hunger Artist," Kafka writes that the guards of the fasting man were "usually butchers, strangely enough." Not so strange, I think.

I know that the world, even if it views me as overweight (and I'm 18 not sure it really does), clearly makes a distinction between me and this very big woman. I would rather stand with her and not against her, see her for all she is besides fat. But I know our experiences aren't the same. My thin friend assumes my fat friend is unhappy because she is fat: therefore, if she loses weight she will be happy. My fat friend has a happy marriage and family and a good career, but insofar as her weight is a source of misery, I think she would be much happier if she could eat her cookie in peace, if people would shut up and leave her weight alone. But the world never lets up when you are her size; she cannot walk to the bank without risking insult. Her fat is seen as perverse bad manners. I have no doubt she would be rid of the fat if she could be. If my left-handedness invited the criticism her weight does, I would want to cut that hand off [. . .].

The predominant biological myth of weight is that thin people 19 live longer than fat people. The truth is far more complicated. (Some deaths of fat people attributed to heart disease seem actually to have been the result of radical dieting.) If health were our real concern, it would be dieting we questioned, not weight. The current ideal of thinness has never been held before, except as a religious ideal; the underfed body is the martyr's body. Even if people can lose weight, maintaining an artificially low weight for any period of time requires a kind of starvation. Lots of people are naturally thin, but for those who are not, dieting is an unnatural act; biology rebels. The metabolism of the hungry body can change inalterably, making it ever harder and harder to stay thin. I think chronic dieting made me gain weight—not only pounds, but fat. This equation seemed so strange at first that I couldn't believe it. But the weight I put back on after losing was much more stubborn than the original weight. I had lost it by taking diet pills and not eating much of anything at all for quite a long time. I haven't touched the pills again, but not eating much of anything no longer works.

When Oprah Winfrey first revealed her lost weight, I didn't envy 20 her. I thought, She's in trouble now. I knew, I was certain, she would gain it back; I believed she was biologically destined to do so. The tabloid headlines blamed it on a cheeseburger or mashed potatoes; they screamed OPRAH PASSES 200 POUNDS, and I cringed at her misery and how the world wouldn't let up, wouldn't leave her alone, wouldn't let her be anything else. How dare the world do this to anyone? I thought, and then realized I did it to myself.

The "Ideal Weight" charts my mother used were at their lowest 21 acceptable-weight ranges in the 1950s, when I was a child. They were based on sketchy and often inaccurate actuarial evidence, using, for the most part, data on northern Europeans and allowing for the most minimal differences in size for a population of less than half a billion people. I never fit those weight charts, I was always just outside the pale. As an adult, when I would join an organized diet program, I accepted their version of my Weight Goal as gospel, knowing it would be virtually impossible to reach. But reach I tried; that's what one does with gospel. Only in the last few years have the weight tables begun to climb back into the world of the average human. The newest ones distinguish by gender, frame, and age. And suddenly I'm not off the charts anymore. I have a place.

A man who is attracted to fat women says, "I actually have less 22 specific physical criteria than most men. I'm attracted to women who weigh 170 or 270 or 370. Most men are only attracted to women who weigh between 100 and 135. So who's got more of a fetish?" We look at fat as a problem of the fat person. Rarely do the tables get turned, rarely do we imagine that it might be the viewer, not the viewed, who is limited. What the hell is wrong with *them*, anyway? Do they believe everything they see on television?

A fashion magazine recently celebrated the return of the "well- 23 fed" body; a particular model was said to be "the archetype of the new womanly woman . . . stately, powerful." She is a size 8. The images of women presented to us, images claiming so maliciously to be the images of women's whole lives, are not merely social fictions. They are *absolute* fictions; they can't exist. How would it feel, I began to wonder, to cultivate my own real womanliness rather than despise it? Because it was my fleshy curves I wanted to be rid of after all. I dreamed of having a boy's body, smooth, hipless, lean. A body rapt with possibility, a receptive body suspended before the storms of maturity. A dear friend of mine, nursing her second child, weeps at her newly voluptuous body. She loves her children and hates her own motherliness, wanting to be unripened again, to be a bud and not a flower.

Recently I've started shopping occasionally at stores for "large women," where the smallest size is a 14. In department stores the size 12 and 14 and 16 clothes are kept in a ghetto called the Women's Department. (And who would want that, to be the size of a woman? We all dream of being "juniors" instead.) In the specialty stores the clerks are usually big women and the customers are big, too, big like a lot of women in my life—friends, my sister, my mother and aunts. Not long ago I bought a pair of jeans at Lane Bryant and then walked through the mall to the Gap, with its shelves of generic clothing. I flicked through the clearance rack and suddenly remembered the Lane Bryant shopping bag in my hand and its enormous weight, the sheer heaviness of that brand name shouting to the world. The shout is that I've let myself go. I still feel like crying out sometimes: Can't I feel satisfied? But I am not supposed to be satisfied, not allowed to be satisfied. My discontent fuels the market; I need to be afraid in order to fully participate [. . .].

The possibility of living another way, living without dieting, began to take root in my mind a few years ago, and finally my second trip through Weight Watchers ended dieting for me. This last time I just couldn't stand the details, the same kind of details I'd seen and despised in other programs, on other diets: the scent of resignation, the weighing-in by the quarter pound, the before and after photographs of group leaders prominently displayed. Jean Nidetch, the founder of Weight Watchers, says, "Most fat people need to be hurt badly before they do something about themselves." She mocks every aspect of our need for food, of a person's sense of entitlement to food, of daring to *eat what we want*. Weight Watchers refuses to release its own weight charts except to say they make no distinction for frame size; neither has the organization ever released statistics on how many people who lose weight on the program eventually gain it back. I hated the endlessness of it, the turning of food into portions and exchanges, everything measured out, permitted, denied. I hated the very idea of "maintenance." Finally I realized I didn't just hate the diet. I was sick of the way I acted on a diet, the way I whined, my niggardly, penny-pinching behavior. What I liked in myself seemed to shrivel and disappear when I dieted. Slowly, slowly I saw these things. I saw that my pain was cut from whole cloth, imaginary, my own invention. I saw how much time I'd spent on something ephemeral, something that simply wasn't important, didn't matter. I saw that the real point of dieting is dieting—to not be done with it, ever.

I looked in the mirror and saw a woman, with flesh, curves, mus- 26 cles, a few stretch marks, the beginnings of wrinkles, with strength and softness in equal measure. My body is the one part of me that is always, undeniably, here. To like myself means to be, literally, shameless, to be wanton in the pleasures of being inside a body. I feel *loose* this way, a little abandoned, a little dangerous. That first feeling of liking my body—not being resigned to it or despairing of change, but actually *liking* it—was tentative and guilty and frightening. It was alarming, because it was the way I'd felt as a child, before the world had interfered. Because surely I was wrong; I knew, I'd known for so long, that my body wasn't all right this way. I was afraid even to act as though I were all right: I was afraid that by doing so I'd be acting a fool.

For a time I was thin. I remember—and what I remember is noth- 27 ing special—strain, a kind of hollowness, the same troubles and fears, and no magic. So I imagine losing weight again. If the world applauded, would this comfort me? Or would it only compromise whatever approval the world gives me now? What else will be required of me besides thinness? What will happen to me if I get sick, or lose the use of a limb, or, God forbid, grow old?

By fussing endlessly over my body, I've ceased to inhabit it. I'm 28 trying to reverse this equation now, to trust my body and enter it again with a whole heart. I know more now than I used to about what constitutes "happy" and "unhappy," what the depths and textures of contentment are like. By letting go of dieting, I free up mental and emotional room. I have more space, I can move. The pursuit of another, elusive body, the body someone else says I should have, is a terrible distraction, a sidetracking that might have lasted my whole life long. By letting myself go, I go places.

Each of us in this culture, this twisted, inchoate culture, has to 29 choose between battles: one battle is against the cultural ideal, and the other is against ourselves. I've chosen to stop fighting myself. Maybe I'm tilting at windmills; the cultural ideal is ever-changing, out of my control. It's not a cerebral journey, except insofar as I have to remind myself to stop counting, to stop thinking in terms of numbers. I know, even now that I've quit dieting and eat what I want, how many calories I take in every day. If I eat as I please, I eat a lot one day and very little the next; I skip meals and snack at odd times.

My nourishment is good—as far as nutrition is concerned, I'm in much better shape than when I was dieting. I know that the small losses and gains in my weight over a period of time aren't simply related to the number of calories I eat. Someone asked me not long ago how I could possibly know my calorie intake if I'm not dieting (the implication being, perhaps, that I'm dieting secretly). I know because calorie counts and grams of fat and fiber are embedded in me. I have to work to not think of them, and I have to learn to not think of them in order to really live without fear [. . .].

I repeat with Walt Whitman, "I dote on myself . . . there is that lot 30 of me, and all so luscious." I'm eating better, exercising more, feeling fine—and then I catch myself thinking, *Maybe I'll lose some weight.* But my mood changes or my attention is caught by something else, something deeper, more lingering. Then I can catch a glimpse of myself by accident and think only: That's me. My face, my hips, my hands. Myself.

9

CAUSE AND EFFECT

ON READING AND WRITING

Stephen King

If you want to be a writer, you must do two things above all others: read a lot and write a lot. There's no way around these two things that I'm aware of, no shortcut. 1

I'm a slow reader, but I usually get through seventy or eighty books a year, mostly fiction. I don't read in order to study the craft; I read because I like to read. It's what I do at night, kicked back in my blue chair. Similarly, I don't read fiction to study the art of fiction, but simply because I like stories. Yet there is a learning process going on. Every book you pick up has its own lesson or lessons, and quite often the bad books have more to teach than the good ones. 2

When I was in the eighth grade, I happened upon a paperback novel by Murray Leinster, a science fiction pulp writer who did most of his work during the forties and fifties, when magazines like *Amazing Stories* paid a penny a word. I had read other books by Mr. Leinster, enough to know that the quality of his writing was uneven. This particular tale, which was about mining in the asteroid belt, was one of his less successful efforts. Only that's too kind. It was terrible, actually, a story populated by paper-thin characters and driven by outlandish plot developments. Worst of all (or so it seemed to me at the time), Leinster had fallen in love with the word *zestful*. Characters watched the approach of ore-bearing asteroids with *zestful smiles*. Characters sat down to supper aboard their mining ship with *zestful anticipation*. Near the end of the book, the hero swept the large-breasted, blonde heroine into a *zestful embrace*. For me, it was the literary equivalent of a smallpox vaccination: I have never, so far as I know, used the word *zestful* in a novel or a story. God willing, I never will. 3

Asteroid Miners (which wasn't the title, but that's close enough) 4
was an important book in my life as a reader. Almost everyone can
remember losing his or her virginity, and most writers can remember
the first book he/she put down thinking: *I can do better than this. Hell,
I am doing better than this!* What could be more encouraging to the
struggling writer than to realize his/her work is unquestionably better than that of someone who actually got paid for his/her stuff?

One learns most clearly what not to do by reading bad prose— 5
one novel like *Asteroid Miners* (or *Valley of the Dolls, Flowers in the
Attic,* and *The Bridges of Madison County,* to name just a few) is worth
a semester at a good writing school, even with the superstar guest
lecturers thrown in.

Good writing, on the other hand, teaches the learning writer 6
about style, graceful narration, plot development, the creation of
believable characters, and truth-telling. A novel like *The Grapes of
Wrath* may fill a new writer with feelings of despair and good old-
fashioned jealousy—"I'll never be able to write anything that good,
not if I live to be a thousand"—but such feelings can also serve as a
spur, goading the writer to work harder and aim higher. Being swept
away by a combination of great story and great writing—of being
flattened, in fact—is part of every writer's necessary formation. You
cannot hope to sweep someone else away by the force of your writing until it has been done to you.

So we read to experience the mediocre and the outright rotten; 7
such experience helps us to recognize those things when they begin
to creep into our own work, and to steer clear of them. We also read
in order to measure ourselves against the good and the great, to get
a sense of all that can be done. And we read in order to experience
different styles.

You may find yourself adopting a style you find particularly 8
exciting, and there's nothing wrong with that. When I read Ray
Bradbury as a kid, I wrote like Ray Bradbury—everything green and
wondrous and seen through a lens smeared with the grease of nostalgia. When I read James M. Cain, everything I wrote came out
clipped and stripped and hardboiled. When I read Lovecraft, my
prose became luxurious and Byzantine. I wrote stories in my teenage
years where all these styles merged, creating a kind of hilarious stew.
This sort of stylistic blending is a necessary part of developing one's
own style, but it doesn't occur in a vacuum. You have to read widely,
constantly refining (and redefining) your own work as you do so. It's
hard for me to believe that people who read very little (or not at all
in some cases) should presume to write and expect people to like

what they have written, but I know it's true. If I had a nickel for every person who ever told me he/she wanted to become a writer but "didn't have time to read," I could buy myself a pretty good steak dinner. Can I be blunt on this subject? If you don't have time to read, you don't have the time (or the tools) to write. Simple as that.

Reading is the creative center of a writer's life. I take a book with 9 me everywhere I go, and find there are all sorts of opportunities to dip in. The trick is to teach yourself to read in small sips as well as in long swallows. Waiting rooms were made for books—of course! But so are theater lobbies before the show, long and boring checkout lines, and everyone's favorite, the john. You can even read while you're driving, thanks to the audiobook revolution. Of the books I read each year, anywhere from six to a dozen are on tape. As for all the wonderful radio you will be missing, come on—how many times can you listen to Deep Purple sing "Highway Star"?

Reading at meals is considered rude in polite society, but if you 10 expect to succeed as a writer, rudeness should be the second-to-least of your concerns. The least of all should be polite society and what it expects. If you intend to write as truthfully as you can, your days as a member of polite society are numbered, anyway.

Where else can you read? There's always the treadmill, or what- 11 ever you use down at the local health club to get aerobic. I try to spend an hour doing that every day, and I think I'd go mad without a good novel to keep me company. Most exercise facilities (at home as well as outside it) are now equipped with TVs, but TV—while working out or anywhere else—really is about the last thing an aspiring writer needs. If you feel you must have the news analyst blowhards on CNN while you exercise, or the stock market blowhards on MSNBC, or the sports blowhards on ESPN, it's time for you to question how serious you really are about becoming a writer. You must be prepared to do some serious turning inward toward the life of the imagination, and that means, I'm afraid, that Geraldo, Keith Obermann, and Jay Leno must go. Reading takes time, and the glass teat takes too much of it.

Once weaned from the ephemeral craving for TV, most people 12 will find they enjoy the time they spend reading. I'd like to suggest that turning off that endlessly quacking box is apt to improve the quality of your life as well as the quality of your writing. And how much of a sacrifice are we talking about here? How many *Frasier* and *ER* reruns does it take to make one American life complete? How many Richard Simmons infomercials? How many whiteboy/fatboy Beltway insiders on CNN? Oh man, don't get me started. Jerry-

Springer-Dr.-Dre-Judge-Judy-Jerry-Falwell-Donny-and-Marie, I rest my case.

When my son Owen was seven or so, he fell in love with Bruce 13 Springsteen's E Street Band, particularly with Clarence Clemons, the band's burly sax player. Owen decided he wanted to learn to play like Clarence. My wife and I were amused and delighted by this ambition. We were also hopeful, as any parent would be, that our kid would turn out to be talented, perhaps even some sort of prodigy. We got Owen a tenor saxophone for Christmas and lessons with Gordon Bowie, one of the local music men. Then we crossed our fingers and hoped for the best.

Seven months later I suggested to my wife that it was time to dis- 14 continue the sax lessons, if Owen concurred. Owen did, and with palpable relief—he hadn't wanted to say it himself, especially not after asking for the sax in the first place, but seven months had been long enough for him to realize that, while he might love Clarence Clemons's big sound, the saxophone was simply not for him—God had not given him that particular talent.

I knew, not because Owen stopped practicing, but because he 15 was practicing only during the periods Mr. Bowie had set for him: half an hour after school four days a week, plus an hour on the weekends. Owen mastered the scales and the notes—nothing wrong with his memory, his lungs, or his eye-hand coordination—but we never heard him taking off, surprising himself with something new, blissing himself out. And as soon as his practice time was over, it was back into the case with the horn, and there it stayed until the next lesson or practice-time. What this suggested to me was that when it came to the sax and my son, there was never going to be any real play-time; it was all going to be rehearsal. That's no good. If there's no joy in it, it's just no good. It's best to go on to some other area, where the deposits of talent may be richer and the fun quotient higher.

Talent renders the whole idea of rehearsal meaningless; when 16 you find something at which you are talented, you do it (whatever *it* is) until your fingers bleed or your eyes are ready to fall out of your head. Even when no one is listening (or reading, or watching), every outing is a bravura performance, because you as the creator are happy. Perhaps even ecstatic. That goes for reading and writing as well as for playing a musical instrument, hitting a baseball, or running the four-forty. The sort of strenuous reading and writing program I advocate—four to six hours a day, every day—will not seem strenuous if you really enjoy doing these things and have an aptitude for them; in fact, you may be following such a program already. If you feel you need permission to do all the reading and writing your little heart desires, however, consider it hereby granted by yours truly.

The real importance of reading is that it creates an ease and inti-17 macy with the process of writing; one comes to the country of the writer with one's papers and identification pretty much in order. Constant reading will pull you into a place (a mind-set, if you like the phrase) where you can write eagerly and without self-consciousness. It also offers you a constantly growing knowledge of what has been done and what hasn't, what is trite and what is fresh, what works and what just lies there dying (or dead) on the page. The more you read, the less apt you are to make a fool of yourself with your pen or word processor.

MEET THE BICKERSONS

Mary Roach

Psychologists have long said it's possible to predict whether a 1
couple will stay happily married simply by looking at how they
fight. This did not bode well for yours truly, who got married earlier
this year. Pretty much all I'd learned about spousal arguing technique came from "The Newlywed Game," which taught us that 1)
the proper form of conflict revolution is to hit your partner over the
head with a large piece of posterboard, and 2) most problems can be
resolved with the acquisition of a brand-new washer and dryer or a
gift pack of Turtle Wax.

I've been told I'm defensive. "Like a cornered mongoose," if I 2
recall correctly, were the exact words. I've also been criticized for
being sarcastic, over-reacting, and crying too easily. I don't deny
these things (though if you were to accuse me of them in the heat of
battle, you can be sure I would, vehemently and with pointy little
teeth bared).

I had a boyfriend who tried to change me. He asked me to use 3
a therapy technique called active listening, a mainstay of modern
marriage counselors for years. It's supposed to make you a more fair,
less combative arguer. I (and here's something you couldn't see coming) objected to this, stating that I was already an active listener. My
ex countered that deep sighs, nostril flares, pacing, and storming
from the room did not qualify. Active listening means focusing carefully on what your partner is saying, very carefully, as though there
were going to be a test, because, in fact, there is. You are required to
paraphrase your beloved's misguided rantings—sorry, feelings—
beginning with the phrase "What I hear you saying is . . ."

I agreed to try it. He went first. Minutes passed. Fortunately, we 4
were on the phone at the time, which allowed me to scribble notes.
He finished and fell silent.

"What I hear you saying," I began, "is that you think I'm defen- 5
sive, and I don't allow you to feel what you're feeling and that makes
you incredibly . . . truncated, wait, flat-footed?"

"Frustrated."   6

"Of course."   7

"You're cheating," he said. "You're writing things down."   8

"Am not." 9

Nothing, not counseling, not even Turtle Wax, was going to save 10 that relationship.

With Ed, I was determined to do things right. I have a friend with 11 a degree in counseling, and I asked her to give me some advice. She encouraged me to use "I" statements rather than "you" statements, because "you" statements put people on the defensive. For instance, one does not say to one's beloved, "You never do the dishes, you self-centered pea brain." One says, "I feel angry and taken advantage of when the people I love leave their dishes for me, especially when it was those people who dirtied them in the first place and ate the leftovers they knew darn well I was planning to have for lunch."

Another suggested technique was "validation," in which each 12 partner makes an effort to endorse the other's feelings, e.g., "I can see why you'd be upset with my failing to wash one small dish and eating an eighth of a taco. I would be too if I were an oversensitive, petty person who only focuses on the negative."

I put all these techniques to work a while back. We were driving, 13 and I had failed to notice a stop sign, which even the most vigilant driver will do from time to time, am I right? Ed did not fail to notice the stop sign, as was evinced by his slamming of the imaginary brakes he has had installed in the passenger side of my car. "When you constantly remark upon my driving irregularities," I began, "I feel scrutinized and inadequate, and by the way, who was it that nearly got us killed by turning into traffic outside Costco?"

Ed was unperturbed by the Costco barb. What got him was the 14 I-feel-blah-dee-blah business. "It's like I'm this horrible person who's hurt you and made you feel awful. Why don't you just get mad and call me a backseat driver, and that'd be that?"

Later that evening I tried to explain what I'd learned about "you" 15 statements and active listening and validating feelings. Ed listened carefully. Then he took my hand in his. "When you talk about things like this, I feel, let me see, like throwing up. How was that?"

Shortly thereafter, Ed left a newspaper clipping on my desk. It 16 described a study at the University of Washington in which 130 newlywed pairs were videotaped arguing and then tracked for six years. It turns out the couples who stayed married had seldom used techniques like active listening and validation, the very techniques the researcher had previously advocated as the path to harmony. He was "shocked and surprised" to find that the happy couples fought like normal people, getting angry, clearing the air, and making up. (Their spats, however, were tinged with soothing and humor.)

This was one instance where I was glad to be proved wrong. So 17 thrilled was I at the prospect of never again having to begin a sentence with "What I hear you saying is" that I made a vow on the spot that the next time Ed got mad at me, I wouldn't get defensive.

It happened on a Saturday afternoon. I had thrown away a set of 18 circa-1970 stereo speakers, when Ed had wanted to keep them because they might come in handy for taking up space in the basement for the next ten years. It didn't go quite the way I'd envisioned. I heard myself lambasting Ed for going through the garbage, checking up on what I'd junked. "You're scrutinizing me again."

Ed looked flabbergasted. "You toss things without even asking 19 me!"

"What's the point? You just say no." 20

"I do not." 21

"Do too." 22

The bell rang, and we withdrew to our corners. Around dinner- 23 time I appeared in the kitchen with the speakers, dusted and polished. Ed, in turn, promised not to supervise my spring cleaning. He asked me to let him know when I caught him checking over or redoing something I'd done. "I'm not even aware of it. So please tell me." He smiled sweetly. "And then I'll deny it."

We're doing just fine, thank you. 24

THE FEAR OF LOSING A CULTURE
Richard Rodriguez

What is culture? 1

The immigrant shrugs. Latin American immigrants come to the 2
United States with only the things they need in mind—not abstractions like culture. Money. They need dollars. They need food. Maybe they need to get out of the way of bullets.

Most of us who concern ourselves with the Hispanic-American 3
culture, as painters, musicians, writers—or as sons and daughters—are the children of immigrants. We have grown up on this side of the border, in the land of Elvis Presley and Thomas Edison; our lives are prescribed by the mall, by the DMV and the Chinese restaurant. Our imaginations yet vascillate between an Edenic Latin America (the blue door)—and the repellent plate glass of a real American city—which has been good to us.

Hispanic-American culture is where the past meets the future. 4
Hispanic-American culture is not an Hispanic milestone only, not simply a celebration at the crossroads. America transforms into pleasure what America cannot avoid. Is it any coincidence that at a time when Americans are troubled by the encroachment of the Mexican desert, Americans discover a chic in cactus, in the decorator colors of the Southwest? In sand?

Hispanic-American culture of the sort that is now showing (the 5
teen movie, the rock song) may exist in an hourglass, may in fact be irrelevant to the epic. The US Border Patrol works through the night to arrest the flow of illegal immigrants over the border, even as Americans wait in line to get into *La Bamba*. Even as Americans vote to declare, once and for all, that English shall be the official language of the United States, Madonna starts recording in Spanish.

But then so is Bill Cosby's show irrelevant to the 10 o'clock news, 6
where families huddle together in fear on porches, pointing at the body of the slain boy bagged in tarpauline—which is not to say that Bill Cosby or Michael Jackson are irrelevant to the future or without neo-Platonic influence. Like players within the play, they prefigure, they resolve. They make black and white audiences aware of a bond that may not yet exist.

Before a national TV audience, Rita Moreno tells Geraldo Rivera   7
that her dream as an actress is to play a character rather like herself:
"I speak English perfectly well . . . I'm not dying from poverty . . . I
want to play *that* kind of Hispanic woman, which is to say, an
American citizen." This is an actress talking, these are show-biz
pieties. But Moreno expresses as well the general Hispanic-American
predicament. Hispanics want to belong to America without betray-
ing the past.

Hispanics fear losing ground in any negotiation with the   8
American city. We come from an expansive, an intimate culture that
has been judged second-rate by the United States of America. For reasons of pride, therefore, as much as of affection, we are reluctant to
give up our past. Hispanics often express a fear of "losing" culture.
Our fame in the United States has been our resistance to assimilation.

The symbol of Hispanic culture has been the tongue of flame—   9
Spanish. But the remarkable legacy Hispanics carry from Latin
America is not language—an inflatable skin—but breath itself, capac-
ity of soul, an inclination to live. The genius of Latin America is the
habit of synthesis.

We assimilate. Just over the border there is the example of   10
Mexico, the country from which the majority of U.S. Hispanics come.
Mexico is mestizo—Indian and Spanish. Within a single family,
Mexicans are light-skinned and dark. It is impossible for the Mexican
to say, in the scheme of things, where the Indian begins and the
Spaniard surrenders.

In culture as in blood, Latin America was formed by a rape that   11
became a marriage. Due to the absorbing generosity of the Indian,
European culture took on new soil. What Latin America knows is
that people create one another as they marry. In the music of Latin
America you will hear the litany of bloodlines—the African drum,
the German accordian, the cry from the minaret.

The United States stands as the opposing New World experi-   12
ment. In North America the Indian and the European stood apace.
Whereas Latin America was formed by a medieval Catholic dream of
one world—of meltdown conversion—the United States was built
up from Protestant individualism. The American melting pot washes
away only embarrassment; it is the necessary initiation into public
life. The American faith is that our national strength derives from
separateness, from "diversity." The glamour of the United States is a
carnival promise: You can lose weight, get rich as Rockefeller, touch
up your roots, get a divorce.

Immigrants still come for the promise. But the United States 13
wavers in its faith. As long as there was space enough, sky enough,
as long as economic success validated individualism, loneliness was
not too high a price to pay (the cabin on the prairie or the Sony
Walkman).

At the beginning of the century, two alternative cultures beckon 14
the American imagination—both highly communal cultures—the
Asian and the Latin American. The United States is a literal culture.
Americans devour what we might otherwise fear to become. Sushi
will make us corporate warriors. Combination Plate #3, smothered in
mestizo gravy, will burn a hole in our hearts.

Latin America offers passion. Latin America has a life—I mean 15
life—big clouds, unambiguous themes, death, birth, faith, that the
United States, for all its quality of life, seems without now. Latin
America offers communal riches: an undistressed leisure, a kitchen
table, even a full sorrow. Such is the solitude of America; such is the
urgency of American need; Americans reach right past a fledgling,
homegrown Hispanic-American culture for the real thing—the darker
bottle of Mexican beer, the denser novel of a Latin American master.

For a long time, Hispanics in the United States withheld from the 16
United States our Latin American gift. We denied the value of assimilation. But as our presence is judged less foreign in America, we will
produce a more generous art, less timid, less parochial. Carlos
Santana, Luis Valdez, Linda Ronstadt—Hispanic Americans do not
have a "pure" Latin American art to offer. Expect bastard themes,
expect ironies, comic conclusions. For we live on the side of the border, where Kraft manufactures bricks of "Mexican style" Velveeta
and where Jack in the Box serves "Fajita Pita."

The flame-red Chevy floats a song down the Pan American Highway: 17
From a rolled-down window, the grizzled voice of Willie Nelson rises in dis-
embodied harmony with the voice of Julio Iglesias. Gabby Hayes and Cisco
are thus resolved.

Expect marriage. We will change America even as we will be 18
changed. We will disappear with you into a new miscegenation.

Along the border, real conflicts remain. But the ancient tear sep- 19
arating Europe from itself—the Catholic Mediterranean from the
Protestant north—may yet heal itself in the New World. For generations, Latin America has been the place—the bed—of a confluence of
so many races and cultures that Protestant North America shuddered
to imagine it.

Imagine it. 20

Acknowledgments

Judy Brady, "Why I Want A Wife," *Ms. Magazine*, 1971. Copyright 1970 by Judy Brady. Reprinted by permission of the author.

Sandra Cisneros, "Only Daughter." Copyright © 1990 by Sandra Cisneros. First published in *Glamour*, November 1990. Reprinted by permission of Susan Bergholz Literary Services, New York. All rights reserved.

Judith Ortiz Cofer, "The Myth of the Latin Women: I Just Met a Girl Named Maria," from *The Latin Deli: Prose & Poetry*. Copyright © 1993 by Judith Ortiz Cofer. Reprinted with the permission of the University of Georgia Press.

Henry Louis Gates, Jr., from *Colored People: A Memoir* copyright © 1994 by Henry Louis Gates, Jr. Used by permission of Alfred A Knopf, a division of Random House, Inc.

Mark Hansen, "E-Mail: What you Should—and Shouldn't—Say." Reprinted with permission of ASSE from *Professional Safety*, Aug. 1999 and the author.

Sue Hubbell, "On the Interstate: A City of the Mind," from *Time*, June 3, 1985. © 1985 Time Inc. Reprinted by permission.

Zora Neale Hurston, "How It Feels to be Colored Me," 1928. Used with the permission of the Zora Neale Hurston Trust.

Garrison Keillor, "How the Crab Apple Grew," from *Leaving Home* copyright © 1987 by Garrison Keillor. Used by permission of Viking Penguin, a division of Penguin Group (USA) Inc. and the author.

Robert D. King, "Should English Be the Law?" © Robert D. King, appeared in *The Atlantic Monthly*, 1997. Used by permission of the author.

Stephen King, from *On Writing: A Memoir of the Craft*. Reprinted with the permission of Scribner, an imprint of Simon & Schuster Adult Publishing Group from *On Writing: A Memoir of the Craft* by Stephen King. Copyright © 2000 by Stephen King.

William Lutz, "Doublespeak," from *Doublespeak*. Copyright © *Doublespeak* by William Lutz. Used by permission by Jean V. Naggar Literary Agency.

N. Scott Momaday, from "The Way to Rainy Mountain." Used by permission of University of New Mexico Press, 1720 Lomas Blvd. N.E., Albuquerque, NM, 87131-1591 U.S.A.

George Orwell, "Shooting an Elephant," from *Shooting an Elephant and Other Essays*, copyright © George Orwell, 1936, copyright 1950 by Harcourt, Inc., and renewed 1979 by Sonia Brownell Orwell. Reprinted by permission of Harcourt, Inc. and Bill Hamilton as the Literary Executor of the Estate of the Late Sonia Brownell Orwell and Secker & Warburg Ltd.

Robert Ramirez, "The Barrio." Used by permission of the author.

Mary Roach, "Meet the Bickersons," first appeared in *Health Magazine*. Reprinted by permission of the author.

Paul Roberts, "How to Say Nothing in Five Hundred Words," from *Understanding English*. Copyright © 1959 by Paul Roberts. Reprinted by permission of Pearson Education, Inc.

Richard Rodriguez, "The Fear of Losing Culture." Copyright © 1988 by Richard Rodriguez. Reprinted by permission of Georges Borchardt, Inc., for the author.

Lawrence J. Schneiderman, "The Ethics of Euthanasia," *Humanist*, 1990. Used by permission of the author.

Brent Staples, "Just Walk On By: A Black Man Ponders His Power to Alter Public Space." Used by permission of the author.

Gloria Steinem, "Sex, Lies, and Advertising," *Ms. Magazine*, Vol. 1, No. 1, 1990. Used by permission of the author.

Amy Tan, "Mother Tongue." Copyright © 1990 by Amy Tan. First appeared in *The Threepenny Review*. Reprinted by permission of the author and the Sandra Dijkstra Literary Agency.